John Pritchard was Bi⋮
in 2014. He was formei
Archdeacon of Canterbuiy. ne nas serveu in parisnes in
Birmingham and Taunton, and was Warden of Cranmer Hall,
Durham. Other books by the author include *The Intercessions
Handbook, Beginning Again, How to Pray, How to Explain Your
Faith, The Life and Work of a Priest, Living Jesus, God Lost and
Found, Living Faithfully, Ten* and *Something More.*

# FIVE EVENTS THAT MADE CHRISTIANITY

*Christmas, Good Friday, Easter,
Ascension and Pentecost*

John Pritchard

First published in Great Britain in 2018

Society for Promoting Christian Knowledge
36 Causton Street
London SW1P 4ST
www.spck.org.uk

*British Library Cataloguing-in-Publication Data*
A catalogue record for this book is available from the British Library

ISBN 978–0–281–07806–6
eBook ISBN 978–0–281–07807–3

1 3 5 7 9 10 8 6 4 2

Typeset by Manila Typesetting Company
First printed in Great Britain by Ashford Colour Press

eBook by Manila Typesetting Company

Produced on paper from sustainable forests

# Contents

# Contents

# 1

## A word at the beginning: what's happened to Christianity's core beliefs?

I looked down at what I was being told was a footprint in the rock from which Jesus had ascended and returned to God one misty morning at the end of his earthly ministry. Really?

It was my first pilgrimage to the Holy Land and it's true that I was prepared to be thrilled at seeing so many places that were special to my faith. But just how gullible did our guide want us to be? We were standing in the courtyard of an ancient Crusader shrine, later taken over by Muslims but still open to Christians, and there in the centre of the octagonal court was a building containing the rock with the incriminating footprint. The members of my party looked at each other in confusion.

Confusion pretty well describes what many Christians experience when asked what they believe about the Ascension. Did Jesus leave the earth at maximum velocity and shoot through the various levels of earth's surrounding atmosphere? Where to? Or did Jesus decide to call it a day and return mysteriously to heaven? In which case, where or what is heaven? Or did Jesus just disappear after a fond farewell, never to be seen again? What do Christians actually believe about the Ascension? Or, let's be personal: what do *I* believe?

It's easy to assume that the central beliefs of the Christian faith are well understood in Britain where this faith has had such a strongly formative influence. Or at least to assume that these beliefs are clearly understood in the Christian community. They aren't. Research repeatedly shows that most people in Britain don't know what happened on Good Friday and Easter Day. To most people the Ascension is a foreign country and Pentecost is simply bizarre. Even the birth of Jesus – good nostalgic material, but what on earth do we mean by saying this baby was also somehow God?

Faced with so many hard questions about these central tenets of the faith, many Christians have become adept at evading them, focusing instead on the more straightforward realities of church life. It's easier to talk about the choice of music, the food bank, and the new vicar than to pin down concepts with technical names like 'incarnation', 'atonement' and 'Second Coming'.

Of course, music is central to worship, the food bank is a crucial part of our care for others, and the new vicar is bound to spring a few surprises, but these are just part of the 'container' of religion in which the glorious mysteries of the faith are supposed to live and breathe and inspire. Religious structures often seem to mask the realities of a living faith, although religion, with its practices, structures, rituals and symbols, is supposed to be a vehicle for faith to do its transformational work, rather than an end in itself.

In any case, there often seems to be a disconnect between the beliefs and trademark activities of Church, and the real-life experience of people struggling to make ends meet, find affordable accommodation, cope with unpredictable friendships, or navigate the blurred boundaries of ethical behaviour in today's complex society. For many of us, life's a building site, and it's hard knowing where to start.

Another problem for a thoughtful person exploring faith is a tendency to find faith reduced to a set of dos and don'ts, musts, oughts and shoulds. Too much religion stays at the preparatory stage of what true faith has to offer, the rules and controls that may later have to be broken, or at least to be more deeply understood. True Christian faith goes beyond that. It looks into the depths, it welcomes questions and embraces doubt, it examines paradox, it relishes 'both/and' more often than 'either/or'. And it focuses on God more than on the things of God. Alas that more of our church life doesn't seem to reflect all this.

But young people especially have seen through much of this play-acting. They realize that the important questions are about the reality of God and the validity of faith, not the church tower appeal and the gyrations of the national Church. If they haven't dismissed the Church as a lost cause, they want to know about the content of the parcel called 'Church', not the rather battered box it's in and the outdated wrapping paper.

Our world is crowded with options, causes, ideas, ideologies and belief systems, so it's not as if people have nowhere else to go. It's rather like my parents' dining room when they retired – crowded with so much furniture it made working your way across the room something of an adventure. And there against the wall was that large French dresser, still thinking it was the best piece in the room, without realizing that few people were looking inside it any more. Does Christianity look too much like that old French dresser?

Have we Christians vacated the central core of our beliefs because it's all too difficult to work out? Have we allowed well-meaning humanism to become the default position for most of our fellow citizens? Many people believe that humanism is the new common ground in society and claim there's a much wider allegiance to this benign gospel of goodwill than shows up in the small membership of the British Humanist Association. Perhaps.

That fine American Bible scholar Walter Brueggemann puts it slightly differently:

> The gospel is a truth widely held, but a truth greatly reduced. It is a truth that has been flattened, trivialized, and rendered inane. Partly, the gospel is simply an old habit among us, neither valued nor questioned. But more than that, our technical way of thinking reduces mystery to problem, transforms assurance into certitude . . . and takes the categories of biblical faith and represents them in manageable shapes. There is then no danger, no energy, no possibility, no opening for newness.[1]

This kind of faith is an old habit that no longer stirs, shocks, confronts or questions either us or a not-waiting world. In the meantime in Western society our souls remain buried alive, awaiting a rescue that can never come from a credit card. A sound comes up from below, a faint tapping, a muffled cry for help. There's life down there. We must listen to what the heart is trying to say, what the soul of society is longing for. The desire for a life with meaning, direction and depth is universal, but

our culture encourages us to rush on to the next elusive pana-
cea, desperately believing that somewhere out there lies happi-
ness. It does, but it isn't simple.

None of us has life sorted. Most of us are confused by the
vast array of challenges and opportunities that press in on us.
In a sense we're all just struggling to get by. But some of us
believe that there are resources in the Christian faith that aren't
being sufficiently used or understood.

There is, therefore, great need for a faith that involves personal experience built on a realistic understanding of what
Christianity is really saying. In this book I will be focusing on
both personal experience and inherited beliefs, but it won't
focus so much on prayer, silence and contemplative practice –
in other words, the direct apprehension of God. I believe those
experiences are vital if the buried soul is to be rescued. But here
I want to suggest that the groundwork of the Christian faith
is reliable and that it makes sense. I want to suggest that those
great Christian beliefs are life-givers.

Those of us who have found the Christian faith compelling
and energizing know that there's an exhilarating story to be
told. I've always been concerned with truth. My first degree was
in law and I believe that the pursuit of truth, mediated through
justice and love, is a first call on anyone's life. I don't want my
life to be based on fantasy, wishful thinking and ignorance – a
claim that atheists sometimes make about Christians. Truth isn't
just a philosophical idea; it places a demand on me to live with
integrity and authenticity, to be true to myself and to others,
and in a sense, to the universe of which I'm a part. In my stu-
dent years I found a faith that made sense to me both intellec-
tually and emotionally, and ever since then I have believed that
if you pursue the truth far enough you'll bump into that enigmatic preacher from Galilee who dared to say that he himself
was 'the way, *the truth*, and the life'.

I've been able to say consistently that the Christian faith
makes more sense of more things, more of the time, than any
other approach to life that I've encountered. This faith adds
me up and subtracts me, it multiplies me and divides me – and
it shows me what the answer to 'me' is. I'm with Archbishop
Justin Welby who often says, 'The best decision that any human

being can ever make in their life, anywhere in the world, in any circumstances, whoever they are, is to follow Jesus Christ as their Lord.'[2] For myself, a life shaped around Jesus Christ and lived consciously in the direction of God is my highest goal.

Like many people, I have been moved to read the account by Paul Kalanithi of his life and approaching death in *When Breath Becomes Air*. Paul was clearly a brilliant neurosurgeon who also had a deep commitment to literature. He was a high-flyer in every respect, and he and his wife made the brave decision to have a baby when they knew Paul wouldn't see much of the baby's life. He wrote out of those depths in which no games-playing makes sense, only rigorous integrity:

> I, like most scientific types, came to believe in the possibility of a material conception of reality, an ultimately scientific world-view that would grant a complete metaphysics, minus outmoded concepts like souls, God, and bearded white men in robes. I spent a good chunk of my twenties trying to build a frame for such an endeavour. The problem, however, eventually became evident: to make science the arbiter of metaphysics is to banish not only God from the world but also love, hate, meaning – a world that is self-evidently *not* the world we live in . . . Science may provide the most useful way to organise empirical, reproducible data, but its power to do so is predicated on its inability to grasp the most central aspects of human life: hope, fear, love, hate, beauty, envy, honour, weakness, striving, suffering, virtue . . . I returned to the central values of Christianity – sacrifice, redemption, forgiveness – because I found them so compelling.[3]

This faith that embraced Paul Kalanithi, and that energizes over two billion people in the world, revolves around the personality of Jesus and the things that happened to him. So I want to take five key events in the life of Jesus, clean off the grime, and suggest credible ways of understanding those events and the beliefs that emerged from them. The events are his birth, the cross, resurrection, Ascension and Pentecost (not technically an event in the personal life of Jesus but clearly a result of it).

Obviously these great events have been written about at enormous length and with much greater wisdom than I could ever manage. The greatest theologians throughout the centuries have unpacked their meaning with superb skill and it would be ridiculous to try to write in that way. I'm not. I'm simply trying to open up these magnificent beliefs in accessible language and show how they can fire up our lives. I want to reveal the Real within the real. These five events have transformed the lives of untold millions of people, past and present. I want to reclaim their power here and now for those of us who, in our own probably quite ordinary way, try to live in the light of Jesus Christ.

Sadly, we're often tempted not to try to live too much of the gospel because we find it just too big, too radical and too demanding. Exploring the unlimited dynamic of the central events of Jesus' life might give us the inspiration to try again.

I was amused to read that the most stressful day in the career of Richard Wilson, formerly cabinet secretary to Prime Minister Tony Blair, was on 9/11 when the United States came under attack from Islamic extremists. Wilson had to make sure that the UK government was prepared for any similar attacks on Britain. Unfortunately he discovered that the Civil Contingencies Unit was away on a staff outing in Yorkshire, the entire Overseas Defence Secretariat was on a bonding exercise in Hertfordshire, and the newly updated government switchboard had crashed. He then asked about the secret escape tunnel out of No. 10 Downing Street. 'It's locked,' came the reply, 'and the man with the key has gone on holiday without telling us where he keeps it.'[4]

It confirms one's worst fears about how history really goes wrong.

But Christians believe that there is a man with a key, and that history isn't just a record of humanity's incompetence and madness. It's also a record of God's patient, ever so patient, interaction with men and women, and of the times when the threads of God's action became so densely packed and alive that a breakthrough took place that changed everything. Five events that changed the world.

With each event I'll first examine what happened, as far as we can grasp it with the limited tools of understanding at our disposal. Then I'll consider what the event means, its 'usable theology' – theology for the person who wants to understand it and journey with it. Then, last, I'll look at what the event means for us today in our following of Jesus Christ and being fed and motivated by these core beliefs. These latter two sections might often seem to overlap, but that's probably healthy – good theology ought to overlap with good practice.

Just one further thought. In each of the five events I start with the contemporary experience of a pilgrim to the holy sites, and on a first visit this is almost always completely bewildering. It's good to be forewarned about this. We arrive inevitably with wonderful images of the holy places generated by a thousand books, films, preachers and storytellers, and the collision with present-day reality can be disorienting and leave us puzzled and unsure how to speak about it to others. That's why a pilgrimage always lives on in the heart of the pilgrim as we continue to process the experience over the coming months and years, integrating the kaleidoscope of impressions with our steady reading of the Gospels. It's hugely stimulating and enriching.

But, of course, we don't need to have been on pilgrimage to the Holy Land to enjoy and receive all the benefits of the five events that made Christianity. God has definitively *done* these things in the life of Jesus Christ and we have the privilege of entering them and being transformed by them, whenever and wherever we live.

My thanks go to my faithful first readers – Dominic Barrington, Gillian Lunn, Sarah Meyrick, Gordon Oliver and my patient wife Wendy. They save me from all errors and in-felicities that I don't keep for myself. Alison Barr, my excellent editor, always keeps me on course. I am grateful to them all.

I have five wonderful grandchildren who I am honoured to love. I want the Christian faith to be as life-giving to them as it has been to me. They probably won't read this book for quite a while – if ever – but this book is for them.

# 2

## *The birth: what happened?*

We shuffled along the south aisle of the ancient church in Bethlehem, an obedient queue of expectant pilgrims from every nation upon earth. That's an exaggeration, but we certainly spoke a lot of different languages. What would we see when we got there, just to the right of the high altar where the queue disappeared?

Not a stable, that's for sure. It was a cave, directly under the altar, 10–15 metres in length, blackened with the soot from a million candles over 17 centuries. And there at one end of the cave was a silver star on the stone floor, illuminated by several hanging lanterns. This was the spot. Nearly everyone knelt down one by one in hurried reverence to kiss the star, the traditional site of the birth of Jesus. I did so too, in a cocoon of my own silence, a moment outside time, a tiny fraction of the centuries of devotion.

I stood up and the noise rose up again and submerged me. Pilgrims chattering, jostling, cameras clicking, videos whirring. Three metres away, behind me, was a tiny chapel where by tradition Mary laid her baby. Manger, the French word for 'to eat', where the cattle munched away, where the Bread of Life was laid.

I crept to the back of the cave and tried to block out the feverish activity at the other end. This was it. Or rather, was this it? No matter; we were within no more than a hundred metres of one of the most celebrated events on earth. I tried to imagine the cave as it might have been, with an exhausted young mother, a proud, protective father, a few random animals, and a group of embarrassed shepherds, tongue-tied but reluctant to leave. And there was a baby in a feeding trough, unconcerned about the fuss, having got through his first wailing protest at this unwelcome exit from a warm, wet home. Now he was sleeping innocently.

I thought a prayer rather than said one, and then we were shovelled out of the cave up the stairs to the church again. This first time I was there the church seemed to be in serious need of repair, which isn't surprising since its origins lie deep in the fourth century when Queen Helena was on her mission to mark the holy sites with Christian shrines. I stood outside and wondered what I'd seen. A couple of times since then I've been in the cave with hardly anyone else there, and silence has enveloped me in timeless awe, but usually I have come away with a strange feeling of having somehow been bruised by the experience. But then, I'm an introvert and like my 'holy moments' to myself.

Then off we go to the Shepherds' Fields. Surely now I'll get the peace, the tranquil fields, the odd fluffy sheep nosing around for good grass, maybe even a sunburnt shepherd leaning on a staff with the little town of Bethlehem in the near distance. Sadly no.

It's true that the Shepherds' Fields are on the edge of the town, but the town threatens to engulf them, and you look out on to a dusty valley over which glowers one of the huge, controversial Israeli settlements. There's a beautiful Franciscan church and a number of outdoor chapels with benches and metal roofs, and a couple of cave chapels where, with a bit of imagination, you can place your watching shepherds that momentous, sonorous night. Once when I was there with a small group, ten of us singing together sounded like a hundred in the superb acoustic of the Franciscan church.

But was this the place? Who knows? And does it matter anyway? You begin to realize that in the Holy Land history and piety overlap, and it's important not to let them get into a fight.

On the other hand, we're left with a number of questions and they make tantalizing food for thought. The birth stories in Luke and Matthew come across very differently. We've got used to a conflated version of events through a thousand cards, carols and retellings of the story, but in some ways it's better to take the two accounts separately.

In Luke the central figure is Mary; in Matthew it's Joseph. Read the accounts again to see how clear that distinction is.

In Luke the main challenge of Jesus inherent in the story is the challenge to Rome, in Matthew it's to Herod. In Luke the angel appears to Mary; in Matthew it's to Joseph, in a dream. The shepherds in Luke are nowhere to be seen in Matthew. On the other hand, the wise men never arrive in Luke, only in Matthew. Herod's terrible massacre of small children goes unrecorded in Luke; but then again, Matthew makes no mention of a 'no vacancies' sign at an inn.

So we have two traditions here, both rich in meaning and not trying to be in conflict, but raising some fascinating questions.

**Question 1: Did Mary and Joseph live in Nazareth or in Bethlehem?** In Luke the early action in the nativity story is in Nazareth. Ah, Nazareth! Another eye-opener. Nazareth was a small farming community of not much more than two or three hundred people, just off the beaten track west of the Sea of Galilee. Today it's a vast urban sprawl with an ancient Christian-Arab heart and a newer Jewish community up the hill. At the centre is an impressive Basilica of the Annunciation, completed only in 1969. You enter a serene space where you look down on to a grotto where tradition has it that the angel appeared to Mary and changed her world. I love to kneel in that gallery, looking down on this holy place, there to muse and pray.

On the altar in that limestone cave are the words '*Verbum caro hic factum est*'. It's all in the '*hic*'. 'The Word was made flesh *here*'. Again, I'm never too bothered whether this is indeed the precise spot, or whether it was somewhere near. The area is pitted with caves that were used as part of the domestic arrangements for houses that needed space for both the family and their animals. Let's assume that it's here, right before our eyes, in this silent grotto. In which case, it's a place with an enormous story to tell.

But let's go back to that question: did Mary and Joseph live here originally or only later after their return from Egypt? Matthew never mentions Nazareth at this point in the story; the only place he mentions in his description of the birth is Bethlehem. Some people think that Luke got carried away with the significance of Galilee and thought that Mary and Joseph must have always lived there, needing to go to Bethlehem only for the census. Then again, Matthew doesn't say they didn't live in Nazareth; he just gives the impression that Bethlehem was their home, before they later transferred to Nazareth for their long-term safety.

But either way, the Gospel record is clear: Bethlehem is the place of the birth, and Nazareth the place where Jesus was brought up.

**Question 2: When did this take place?** Luke is usually given the nod in this debate because he's so concerned with particularity. God chose a particular time (the days of King Herod), with a particular Emperor (Augustus), a particular Governor (Quirinius), a particular place (Bethlehem) and a particular person (Mary). The trouble is that there are other known historical facts that confuse this straightforward dating of the birth. Luke says that the whole world was to be taxed (Luke 2.1), but there is no record of a census of the whole empire at any time. There was, however, a census in Judea (not Galilee) in AD 6 after Herod Archelaus of Judea was deposed by Augustus and Quirinius was put in as Governor from AD 6 to 12. The Emperor wanted to know what the pickings in Judea would be like, and Quirinius went off to find out by means of a census. Was this the census that Luke was referring to?

The other confusing factor, biblical scholar Paula Gooder says, is that:

> Roman censuses were done by household, and the main requirement was simply that you had to be at home. Galilee was in a different region under the control of Herod Antipas, so if Joseph had lived there [in Nazareth] there would have been no conceivable point in his travelling to Judea [to Bethlehem] since his taxes would have been paid in Galilee, not in Judea.[1]

Luke's account of the census is therefore odd in at least two respects – empire-wide censuses didn't seem to occur, and any local census that did happen required local residence, not travel to another part of the country.

So what are we to conclude? Perhaps, say some scholars, there was an earlier census of both Galilee and Judea while

Herod the Great (who died in 4 BC) was still alive and the country still united. And people may then have had to register in a different way, that is, in their ancestral town rather than where they now lived. Luke may have confused this census with the famous one of Quirinius in AD 6. It's a possibility, and that would locate the birth around 5 BC, before the death of Herod and, interestingly, at a time when Chinese records show that there was a major comet in the night sky – indeed, a 'tailed' comet that appeared in the East and was visible for around seventy days and could have given the impression of being a 'guiding' star.[2]

Another suggestion is that Luke was puzzled as to why a Jesus who lived in Nazareth would be born in Bethlehem, so he used a bit of poetic licence and offered a census as the explanation. But that suggestion doesn't sit well with Luke's characteristic concern for accuracy. I think I prefer the possibility of Luke being confused about two different censuses.

**Question 3: Where's the stable?** I give ground to no one in relishing the drama of a young woman in the early stages of labour desperately needing somewhere to stay for the imminent birth and having to settle for a stable because there was no room in the rowdy, overcrowded inn. Unfortunately the facts don't stack up. The Greek word for 'inn' which Luke uses when he says that there was no room is '*kataluma*', and this word is only used elsewhere in the Gospels to describe a guest room, never an inn, for which the word used is '*pandocheion*' (as in the parable of the Good Samaritan; compare Luke 2.7 and 10.34). *Kataluma*, interestingly, is used by Luke in his description of the 'guest room' in which Jesus met his disciples for the Last Supper.

The picture we have, then, is probably more like this: the house to which Joseph and Mary came was the family home in Bethlehem but because so many of the extended family were visiting for the census, there was 'no room in the *kataluma*', the guest room, or the guest section of the single family space. In a rural town like Bethlehem the family may well have lived in a building above a cave kept for the animals, occupying, as it were, the mezzanine level of a single structure. Mary therefore gave birth in the cave level of the building and placed her child in the animals' feeding trough (suitably cleaned, one hopes).

So Mary and Joseph have been given the greatest responsibility imaginable, to nurture, protect, teach and love the Son of God. It's a staggering thought. But at this point they were simply a newly engaged/betrothed couple amazed at the miracle of birth, exhausted but full of wonder. As with every couple at this moment, they would have been as vulnerable as the child they had brought into the world. The baby's defencelessness would have overturned all their own certainties, except the certainty of love.

**Question 4: What do we make of the wise men?** Another much loved part of our nativity play is the appearance of the wise men, copiously adorned in rich curtain material and gaudy crowns, perhaps with a camel or two if the teachers have been particularly enterprising. But how did they become kings? Come to that, how did they get numbered at three? Generations before us have done their best to find an equivalent to the idea of 'magi' and kings seemed about right. Moreover, three gifts are mentioned, gold, frankincense and myrrh, so three kings seemed a good number too.

Magi were celebrities in the Middle East. They were the clever Nobel prize-winners of their day. Technically they were members of the priestly caste from the Medes and Persians with particular skill in interpreting dreams, but by this time they were also astrologers with the ability to read the stars. Later they were to descend to the realms of sorcerers, quacks and con artists, but at this time they were still held in high esteem. And yet they laid their wisdom at the feet of a baby.

The magi were, of course, Gentiles, so here in these two accounts of the birth we have two groups of outsiders being the first to welcome Jesus: the shepherds from the bottom of the heap in Jewish society, and the magi from the world beyond Judaism entirely. Already we see how the good news embodied in this tiny infant was for the whole world, top to bottom and side to side. Here is a universal hope in the surreal garb of swaddling clothes.

What on earth is God thinking of?

**Last question (the one I've been putting off): Was Mary a virgin?** My problem here is that I always lean towards being orthodox in my beliefs, but you can only believe what you can believe and I'm genuinely puzzled by this one. Let's look at the background.

Mary and Joseph were 'betrothed'. This was rather more than 'engaged', though that word will do if we want to avoid confusing people even more about this unusual birth. Betrothal was the first stage of marriage. It was more than engagement, which is a preliminary agreement. Betrothal involved the drawing up of a deed and the exchange of money, but it didn't allow sexual intercourse. So to be pregnant in the year of betrothal was unacceptable enough, but to be pregnant and not by her husband-to-be would have been socially catastrophic.

Luke makes it pretty clear that he intends us to know that Mary was a virgin. 'Gabriel was sent by God to a town in Galilee called Nazareth, to a virgin engaged to a man whose name was Joseph' (1.26–27). Later Luke emphasizes the point as Mary says, 'How can this be, since I am a virgin?' (1.34). Most scholars seem to think that Mary might not have been more than 12 or 13, because this was the normal age for marriage, but also because culturally it would have been harder to guarantee virginity much older than that. Luke is quite clear that Mary is a virgin.

So is Matthew. Or at least, he's sure that Joseph isn't the human father. 'Joseph, being a righteous man and unwilling to expose her to public disgrace, planned to dismiss her quietly' (Matthew 1.19). It took an angel to stop him. Matthew too believed in the divine conception of Jesus and that Mary was a virgin.

Matthew quotes Isaiah at this point, demonstrating that the birth of Jesus fulfilled the prophecy in 7.14 that 'the virgin shall conceive, and bear a son, and shall call his name Immanuel' (KJV). It's often pointed out that the Hebrew word used in Isaiah is '*almah*', meaning a young woman, and not necessarily a virgin. But the whole thrust of both Matthew and Luke is that Jesus was conceived without human action. (There is, of course, no birth narrative in either Mark or John.) What we have to decide for ourselves is how definitive their interpretation of the birth really is. We must have a bias towards the convictions of Scripture but the task of interpretation still lies with us.

Now, these Gospel writers were addressing a first-century audience, not a twenty-first-century one. What was it they were trying to convince their audience about? It was surely that this was no ordinary child, but God's own. If so, this child obviously couldn't have a human father. QED. But a twenty-first-century mind is entitled to ask, 'Is a virgin birth necessary to ensure that Jesus was divine?' Jesus could be seen as divine by a number of different routes, not just one. There's quite a range of theological positions, all of which maintain the divinity of Jesus but express it in a variety of ways, some of which we'll explore later.

When it comes down to it, therefore, we have to ask ourselves what makes most sense to us with the information and understanding we have. The traditional teaching is that the virgin birth was just as Luke and Matthew present it. The key theological point, however, is that their accounts are intended to make clear that Jesus was divine. The important thing is not to let the virgin birth be a litmus test to decide who is acceptable to orthodox Christianity and who isn't. The virgin birth will always be a mystery among the many mysteries we face in our limited grasp of God's action in the world.

To go to Bethlehem today is to be faced with lots of questions, many of them political. A wall cuts off the town from the thrusting self-confidence of Jerusalem. Today, Mary and Joseph could not have walked straightforwardly to the Temple to present Jesus there and to encounter those two devout, maverick figures of Simeon and Anna. They would have been held up, possibly for hours, at the checkpoint that is guarded by heavily armed young soldiers. Indeed, one of the popular postcards in Bethlehem today is the back view of a couple – the young woman on a donkey holding a baby – standing before a huge gash in a wall with the holy city beyond. May it be so.

In the meantime we present-day pilgrims come here to Bethlehem and are jolted uncomfortably out of the more sentimental pictures we might have had of a rural backwater where, above its deep and dreamless sleep, the silent stars go by. Nevertheless, the hopes and fears of all the years still meet there, for this is where Jesus was born, and he is our morning star.

# 3

## *The birth: what does it mean?*

We've looked at what happened at the birth of Jesus and explored some of the likely scenarios. But what does it really mean? Why do we see this birth to a peasant girl in a backwater of the Roman Empire two millennia ago as so groundbreaking? Why do we cover it with the heavy-sounding word 'incarnation' and why have some of the best minds in history made it their life's work to explore it? Here are some of the many meanings of what happened, and what was started, that momentous night in a cave in Bethlehem.

### We know what God is like

I was once talking with some primary schoolchildren about God. 'How old is he?' one little girl asked. 'Very old,' I said. 'A million years?' she persisted. 'More than that,' I said. 'God has always been alive.' She pondered this information for a while and then announced solemnly, 'He must need a bath soon.'

Quite understandably, we have always had difficulty in saying anything remotely adequate about the nature of God. We've tried using the Bible's own categories, such as God saying to Moses at the burning bush, 'I am who I am' (Exodus 3.14), but that's hardly been crystal clear. We've looked to John's delightfully simple declaration that 'God is love' (1 John 4.16) and found that helpful, if still somewhat opaque. A famous argument of St Anselm in the eleventh century was that God is 'that than which nothing greater can be conceived'. St Thomas Aquinas called God the First Mover and First Cause. In the twentieth century there was a popular move to describe God as the Ground of Being. Of course, the truth is that mere human beings are no more going to be able to offer a coherent description of God than Harry Potter is of J. K. Rowling, because they exist in entirely different dimensions of reality. So we have often looked for metaphors instead: God as Ultimate Reality, Gentle Persuader, Shimmering Presence, Aching Beauty.

In other words, the human search to understand God is serious and perennial but ultimately bound to fail. We are creatures not the Creator, frustrating as that is to those who like to construct a parody of God so they can knock it down. The basic problem, of course, is that God is nothing – in the sense that God is 'no thing', not a single object in a field of objects. In a Christian understanding of God you can't talk about God among a number of 'things' – like the Statue of Liberty, rice pudding, Napoleon, an umbrella, and God. God is not a thing like that, but rather the divine reality undergirding everything that exists. (There we go, defining again. And by the way, I apologize for sometimes using 'he' for God. God is beyond gender but I find that avoidance of the personal pronoun often leads to ugly expressions such as 'Godself'.)

So you could say: the universe minus God equals nought; God minus the universe equals God. The universe (or universes if we're to believe our astro-physicists) exists in God, not the other way round.

But if this is humanity's problem, so too was it God's problem. How would God be able to make 'himself' understood by the inhabitants of earth? God had given humankind excellent guidance on how to live and flourish. It was in the Ten Commandments and the wider law of Moses, but it hadn't worked too well. Then God had sent the best kind of king he could find (David), but that experiment hadn't lasted either. Then God had sent the prophets with a message of both warning and promise, but they kept on being ignored or killed. What was God to do?

The answer was Jesus, that baby in a feeding trough in Bethlehem. If you're going to make yourself understood by humans then you have to use human categories to achieve it. Nothing else will convince people. God isn't a theory to be proven or an energy to be discussed. The American Franciscan Richard Rohr puts it like this:

In the biblical tradition we only seem to know God by relating to God face to face, almost as if God refuses to be known apart from love. It's all about relationship. As Martin Buber, the Jewish philosopher and mystic, put it 'All real living is meeting'.[1]

Of course, God isn't limited to personhood. How could God be at all limited when God is the source of all being, animal, vegetable and mineral? But God can't truly be understood by human beings in anything less than human shape. So he gave us the ultimate demonstration of what divinity is, one that *embodied* the reality it revealed. That's why we call this event the 'incarnation', from the Latin *in caro*, 'in the flesh'.

Christians believe that Jesus is the human face of God, God's self-portrait. Metaphors give us our best descriptors: Jesus is the body language of God, the parable of God, God's autobiography, the composer who finally steps on to the stage to play the solo part. God did what no novelist could do: he entered the story and became one of the characters. In a famous phrase attributed to Archbishop Michael Ramsey, 'God is Christlike, and in him is no unChristlikeness at all.' Or as another bishop theologian, David Jenkins, saw it, 'God is as he is in Jesus; and therefore there is hope.'[2] To complete a trinity of episcopal theologians, Rowan Williams puts it like this:

> Here is a human life so shot through with the purposes of God, so transparent to the action of God, that people speak of it as God's life 'translated' into another medium. Here God is supremely and uniquely at work.[3]

Paul is succinct: 'He is the image of the invisible God . . . For in him all the fullness of God was pleased to dwell' (Colossians 1.15, 19).

Of course, there's a wide spectrum of understandings about how Jesus could be the human face of God. At one end of the spectrum (top down) Jesus Christ is the second person of the Trinity, eternally God, the Word who existed before creation and who was instrumental in creation itself. This is the Christ of the Nicene creed: 'God from God, Light from Light, true God from true God, begotten, not made.' At the other end of the spectrum (bottom up) Jesus is the one human being who was completely conscious of God's presence in his life and who responded fully to that presence moment by moment. He was the ultimate human being, someone who lived so close to God and was so saturated in God that very soon people who had known him were saying he must have been the 'Son of God'; no other description seemed to fit.

In between those two ends of the spectrum – top down and bottom up – are innumerable gradations of understanding that have kept both theologians and ordinary believers busy for centuries. The whole spectrum of beliefs can claim to be orthodox theology, though it's clearly possible to tip over the edge at one end or the other, so that Jesus become 'too much just God' or 'too much just human'.

There is a danger, however, that these ways of thinking about Jesus are too static and keep him frozen in time, pinned to the wall of our imaginations. Better perhaps to think of the life of Jesus as a video of the activity of God. Here is this deeply attractive but puzzling figure, moving through life voicing the thoughts and enacting the behaviour of God in the way he loved and healed, taught and forgave, encouraged and challenged. Here was God in Christ confronting evil, submitting on the cross to the wretched judgement of desperate men, and rising again to reveal the ultimate victory of love. It's this story of Jesus, human life as it could be lived, demonstrated in full colour and beauty, that has proved irresistible to millions of people through the centuries. They've glimpsed – *I've* glimpsed – the outline of God.

Of course, this figure of Jesus is bound to be complex and enigmatic as well as compelling and endlessly fascinating. How could it be otherwise if he does indeed bring divine reality into focus? Men and women have seen so many different Jesuses and it's made for continuous debate and considerable controversy. Take these two descriptions, for example. The first is a favourite of mine from a former Lord Chancellor, Lord Hailsham, in his book *The Door Wherein I Went*:

> I looked at the gospel again, and quite suddenly a new portrait seemed to stare at me out of the pages. I had never

previously thought of a laughing, joking Jesus, physically strong and active, fond of good company and a glass of wine, telling funny stories, using, as every good teacher does, paradox and exaggeration ... applying nicknames to his friends and holding his companions spellbound with his talk. As I reflected on this I came to the conclusion that we should have been absolutely entranced by his company.[4]

I recognize all that, and find it very attractive. But here is a description I saw in New Zealand on a poster in a remarkable centre working for peace, justice and the well-being of the environment:

Jesus was a radical, non-violent teacher who hung around with crooks, prostitutes and lepers. He never spoke English. He was anti-wealth, anti-death penalty, anti-public prayer – but was never anti-gay, never mentioned abortion or birth control, and never called the poor lazy, never justified torture, never fought for tax cuts for the wealthiest Nazarenes. He was a long haired, brown skinned, homeless, community organising, Middle Eastern Jew.

You may recognize a difference of emphasis ...

There's a final issue. I was once leading a retreat and talking to individuals about what was on their minds. One afternoon an intelligent, thoughtful woman said to me, 'I get God. I can imagine God as the divine presence in all things. But I just can't see where Jesus fits in.' Shortly afterwards I was in another conversation and a faithful Christian woman said, 'I get Jesus. Jesus has always been part of my life. But I just can't get God; God is too big.' Which end of the divine paradox do we come in from?

It might help to think of being in a house with no windows. We go from room to room getting more desperate to see what's out there and for light to come into this darkened world. Finally we stumble into a room on the ground floor with a huge window through which light is pouring as if from creation itself. We look through the window and see a view so stunning it's almost unbearable. We know that this is what we were made for, to be part of this breathtaking landscape, but part of us fears we might get lost in the vast expanse out there, overwhelmed by its beauty. What shall we do – stay inside and look through the window so that we're able to feast on that marvellous view, or shall we venture through that window and try to participate in the glory that's out there?

The choice is ours and both ways are equally exciting. Some of us will approach the immense mystery of God through the window of Jesus, happily able to see and understand as much of God as we can manage without blowing a fuse. Others of us will want to climb out of the window (it turns out to be a patio door!) and seek to be united with the breathtaking beauty of God directly. Neither way is better than the other. We may indeed find ourselves going in and out of that window at different times. God takes our individuality with joyful seriousness and has provided for us all.

The glorious truth is simply this: because of Jesus we know, as much as human beings can, what God is like.

## We know that God is with us, for us, on our side

We were visiting Mary's well in Nazareth. This is another of those special spots where you feel you're really within touching distance of Jesus. There's a Crusader crypt in a Greek Orthodox church guarding the original village water supply. I stood watching pilgrims taking some water from the ancient well, and suddenly in my imagination I saw a young mother with a tousle-headed child doing the same. The little chap was trying to be helpful but he was very small. Mary and Jesus must have come here for water.

Through the incarnation we can be confident that God knows in all its depth what it's like to be human. God is with us in the warp and weft of ordinary life. God is thoroughly on our side, committed to our well-being, encouraging us to live as fully and effectively as we can. God is no remote deity watching from afar – not that he ever was – but now we can be sure that God has the inside story on being human, with all the knowledge, the limitations, the emotions, the highs, lows, hopes, fears of every human being.

Have we thought this through? Think of those hidden years growing up in Nazareth. Can you hear him learning how to talk, the early gibberish, his parents delighting at his first words?

Can you see a little boy chasing around the village and hurrying home when the rain started to pour down? Can you see him falling over, clutching his bleeding knee, and his mother rushing out to comfort him? Can you see him getting angry when another child cheats in the game they're playing in the back field? Can you see him trying to get to sleep but worried that he hadn't finished that job in the workshop properly, or learnt that bit of the Torah?

As he grew up Jesus must have experienced the full range of human emotions, love of his family and anxiety about illness, joy as they danced at weddings and festivals, and sorrow when friends in the village died. He would probably have been cautious, perhaps even fearful, of the brutal Romans. Did he ever get depressed? As he entered his teens he must presumably have known adolescent crushes and sexual urges. What did he do with them? Perhaps he fell in love but agonizingly decided he had to put the idea of marriage aside because he couldn't shake off the growing conviction that there was something else he had to do. If we're serious about what incarnation means then these human emotions must have been part of the deal.

God understands work from the inside too. God knows about the anxiety of getting work, paying bills and taxes, the way that random events can wipe out your savings. He knows about the precariousness of life, especially on the margins among the poor. As the oldest son Jesus might have had to take over the family business when Joseph died. He probably cut down trees, shifted heavy logs back to the workshop, fashioned planks for doors and lintels, got splinters in his hands, hit his thumb with his hammer (and said what?). A builder had to be tough. He understood work.

So we now know that God is with us in all we are and do, with us in the sense of knowing, understanding and wanting the best for us at every point. That word 'with' is very important. Sam Wells encourages us to believe that it's probably the most important word in the Gospel.[5] He points out that the first 30 years of Jesus' life were just spent being with us, and only out of that 'with-ness' could come what Jesus did 'for' us – though even on the cross, at the deepest level, Jesus was simply showing us what God's love for us is like, how far God will go to be *with us* in everything.

I always find it interesting how little words are often very significant in the Bible. That word 'with' is one of them. 'But' is another; things are as they are and may seem to be dire, 'but' with God that's never the end of the story (e.g. Romans 5.8; 1 Peter 2.9). 'In' is similar; it's being 'in Christ' that defines our identity and our hope. '*En Christo*' is a phrase repeated 216 times in the letters of Paul (e.g. Romans 8.1; 2 Corinthians 5.17). Here, however, we are concerned with that word 'with', and 'with' is fundamental to our understanding of what the incarnation means. Embedded in Isaiah and picked up by Matthew is the promise we examined earlier, 'The young woman [virgin] is with child and shall bear a son, and shall name him Immanuel' (Isaiah 7.14). That word Immanuel means 'God is with us.'

God is indeed with us, for us, on our side, and nothing will ever shake that absolute solidarity.

## We know what it is to be human

Every so often I ask myself who I know, or have known, who most helpfully fills in the picture for me of what a full and rounded human being can be. Who seems most alive, rooted, wise, at peace, comfortable in being themselves? Who enriches my life just by meeting me and talking with me? Who makes me feel that goodness is possible? The answer is often surprising. It's not usually the most successful, well off or well travelled. It's more likely to be someone who's seen quite a bit of life, who listens a lot, thinks deeply, makes insightful observations, and has probably been wounded and recovered. It may be someone who in the world's eyes is quite hidden. Who do you know, or have you known, who you think understands most about being human?

With the life of Jesus, not only does God know how to be human, so do we. In Jesus we have a model to shape ourselves around, because here we see a human life as it could be, full of grace and truth. This is the original design, the blueprint, what we have the potential to be – *but not just by trying harder.* That route to human perfection has always been a religious temptation. Try harder, pray harder, confess more, work more, give more – and it's all death-dealing. It induces guilt and failure and cripples our understanding of grace. It's another form of the ancient heretical path of trying to earn our way into God's favour. The gospel doesn't work like that; it's good news, not bad advice.

How it actually works is how it worked for Jesus. Jesus didn't try harder to be good; *he was good because he was united to his Father at the core of his being.* It was being in union with God that enabled him to live with such freedom, humility and authenticity. Quite simply, our goal needs to be to have 'more of God' rather than 'more of ourselves', greater closeness with God rather than greater effort from our already weary selves. That way we can begin to live more fully the humanity that God offers us and has demonstrated in Jesus.

Historically, Christians have often reduced the glory of religion to a set of requirements for heaven, with the marking scheme of 'half marks and you're in'. Indeed, sometimes religion has gone a stage further and set about creating guilt so that it can then forgive it. Religion then becomes a form of sin-management rather than the transformation of human life into what Jesus called 'life in all its fullness'. Healthy religion will always create a bigger, richer picture of what life is and what it's for. Unhealthy religion will diminish it. Ask this question of any expression of religious faith that you come across: is its vision of life bigger or smaller than it would be without it?

Former Archbishop of Canterbury William Temple once said that if someone told him to write plays like Shakespeare, he would answer that Shakespeare could do that but he couldn't. And if someone told him to live a life like Jesus, he would say that Jesus could do it but he couldn't. But if the spirit of Shakespeare were to come and live in him then he could write plays a bit like the great playwright. And if the Spirit of Jesus were to live in him, then he could begin to live a little bit like Jesus. It's all about being united with God in openness and trust.

Because of Jesus we know what it is to be human. And that starts with claiming the dignity of our humanity. In the film *I, Daniel Blake*, Daniel is in a job centre and has been treated in a deeply demoralizing and depersonalized way. He stands up and in protest declares loudly that he is not a client, a customer or a service user; that he's not a shirker, a scrounger, a beggar or a thief; that he's not a national insurance number, or a blip on a screen. He protests to the astonished audience that he has paid his dues in full and was proud to do so, but that he doesn't tug the forelock and is glad to look his neighbour in the eye and help him if he can. And he doesn't seek or accept charity. He comes to a splendid climax by declaring simply that his name is Daniel Blake, and he is a man and not a dog. And as such, he demands his rights, and that he be treated with respect. He is Daniel Blake, a citizen, nothing more and nothing less. He ends with a dignified 'thank you', leaving the job centre stunned.

It's a fine statement of our inalienable value as human beings. God has treated us with breathtaking respect by taking on our humanity. 'The Word became flesh and lived among us, and we have seen his glory' (John 1.14). Our dignity lies in the fact that we are created in the image and likeness of God, and in the further fact that in Jesus God has inhabited human life beautifully. We see the glory of God in a human life opened fully to God. The second-century Bishop of Lyon, St Irenaeus, famously wrote, 'The glory of God is a human being fully alive.' We've seen it in Jesus; now we can all aspire to it.

And it's important to affirm the physicality of Jesus and therefore of our humanity. There has often been in Christianity an unfortunate tendency to locate evil in our bodiliness, so that shame gets associated with sex, alcohol, obesity, body image and so on. These can be important factors in our unhappiness but God is telling us in Jesus that although we can abuse our bodies to our detriment, it's good to be a body. Let's start there, with our created-ness and the significance of Jesus, rather than by associating the body with evil and shame. And by the way, Jesus says that it's the hidden attitudes of greed, hypocrisy, pride and self-centredness that are far more destructive of our humanity than the problems we get into with our bodies.

In Jesus we've caught a glimpse of what it really means to be human. And it's good.

## The birth of Jesus means that the material world matters

I love the materiality of Jesus. He doesn't float around dreamily looking to the heavens, thinking holy thoughts. He immersed himself completely in the material world, knew it from the inside and drew his teaching out of 30 years of Galilean experience. Out of his work as a builder he spoke of sawdust and pieces of wood that got in people's eyes, of poor building foundations, dishonest managers, and workers who wasted their talents. Out of the celebrations and sadnesses of village life he spoke of weddings and bridesmaids, of funerals and bereavement rituals. Out of living in a farming culture he spoke about ploughing, and sowing and reaping, soil types, weeds and wheat, sheep that got lost, barns and weather forecasting. Out of living in an occupied and often violent land he spoke about armed robbery and military strategy. Out of living in a simple house where the kitchen was the heart of the home he spoke about yeast, bread, salt, garden herbs and – wistfully perhaps – he spoke a lot about banquets. Out of his experience of family life he drew stories of sons who ran away and then returned, of jealous brothers, widows who had to marry their brothers-in-law, and families tucked up in bed when neighbours banged on the door.

Jesus' physical environment gave him the raw material for his teaching.

I was once in Bethlehem at the inspirational International Centre when its director, Lutheran pastor Mitri Raheb, said that visitors often asked when his family had first come to the Holy Land, not believing that this highly educated Christian Arab could be a native of the land himself. Mitri Raheb said, 'Well, my great, great, great, great, great, great, great, great (etc.) grandmother might well have been Jesus' babysitter.' Jesus had a babysitter? Why not? It's all part of the real, material world that Jesus inhabited and is therefore loved and 'owned' by God.

The material world matters, and not just for parables and sermon illustrations. God has inhabited this beautiful and messy world. He has honoured it by embracing it, so nothing in future can truly be called 'secular'. We have done great harm to religion by maintaining a divide between the sacred and the secular, as if God is involved in the one but is suspicious of the other. Every part of life belongs to God, who creates and sustains the heavens and the earth. This surely lays an absolute requirement on Christians to care for the earth and to make environmental issues a vital expression of obedience to the gospel. 'The earth is the LORD's and all that is in it, the world, and those who live in it' (Psalm 24.1). 'Loving our neighbour' involves loving our neighbour's grandchildren who will inherit a prospering or ravaged earth.

God gives a wholehearted affirmation to matter, the unruly stuff of which everything is made. There's no part of creation with a sign over it that says 'keep off the grass'. The material world and the spiritual world are fundamentally integrated. Matter is the scaffolding, or hiding place, of spirit.

I like the way this was demonstrated in an incident from the ministry of the saintly Bishop of Lincoln, Edward King (1829–1910). A parish priest was trying to explain to the bishop how frustrated he got trying to prepare his parishioners for taking Holy Communion. 'I explained it to one farm worker, and then asked him what he did to prepare for Communion, and he said, "I clean my boots." It's hopeless!' 'That man,' said the wise bishop, 'was doing the best thing he could to prepare for taking Communion.'

The material and the spiritual must not be consigned to separate spheres when we have a God who has revealed himself in the most vivid, tangible way imaginable, the physicality of a baby in a feeding trough.

Take that a stage further and we see that if the physical is the doorway to the spiritual, the finite revealing the infinite, then earth is the doorway to heaven. We don't need to become fluffy spiritual romantics to discern the shape of the kingdom or the contours of heaven. Heaven starts right here and now. This is where God is. All we have to do is accept that discernment and respond to the invitation.

Bishop Stephen Verney put the invitation like this: 'God the Father, God the Son, God the Holy Spirit, request the pleasure of your company at the marriage of the Love of God to Human Nature. RSVP.'

RSVP indeed.

# 4

## The birth:
## what does it mean for us now?

So we've looked at what happened in this momentous birth and we've thought about what it means in a straightforward theology of the incarnation. The question now is what all this means for our discipleship as we follow Christ today. How does the marvellous story of God's dazzling love give us a surge of grace that makes a lasting difference to us and to others? I'm going to pick out a few of the ways that occur to me, realizing that I will only be scratching the surface of the implications of the incarnation.

### It means that Christmas is the feast of the outsider

We were driving up from Jericho to Jerusalem, 3,000 feet of steady ascent, reversing the journey of Jesus' parable of the Good Samaritan, and doing it in much greater comfort in our modern tourist coach. As I looked out of the window I could see groups of untidy tents and awnings, tethered goats and scattered signs of domesticity. Bedouin, ancient occupiers of the land. Were these the shepherds who came from their fields at night to find in the city of David a Saviour, who is Christ, the Lord?

We might have tended to look out from our air-conditioned coach and thought of the Bedouin as unfortunate wanderers, having to live on the edge of society without modern facilities (though they all have their mobile phones). We might have felt sorry for them and wondered how they managed. But of course, we couldn't have been more wrong. They are today's equivalents of the ones who saw and heard what the rest of us long for. They are like the chosen ones who, that starlit night, found themselves gazing at a God with DNA and fingerprints.

These were just like the outsiders who became the highly favoured insiders.

Christmas is the feast of the outsider, as the Bedouin shepherds made clear. The wise men were outsiders of a different sort. They were Gentiles, non-Jews, coming from way beyond the promised land and the people of the promise. But they too were the ones invited to witness that moment of truth when the eternal Word of all times and places became flesh at one time and one place. In our twenty-first-century arrogance we think that wise men come from the West. Hardly. Wise men came first from the East.

Lots of people in the wealthy West approach Christmas with a set of attitudes ranging from nostalgia to hedonism. The first adverts for Christmas dinners and holiday packages appear outside pubs and hotels in August. The Christmas juggernaut then gains speed throughout the autumn until it reaches mild hysteria by mid-December. Credit cards are red-hot with overuse. Parties are occasions for unfortunate events, later regretted and best forgotten. Career drinkers are out in force. Everything is in excess.

Apologetically, people then remember that there are outsiders too at Christmas, and money is donated to homeless charities, and ancient relatives, forgotten for most of the year, get invited to Christmas dinner. But really it's outsiders who should take pride of place at Christmas, as did the Bedouin shepherds and the wise foreigners from the East.

I went from six years in the rarefied atmosphere of Oxford and Cambridge to serve a curacy in the centre of Birmingham. The move was hugely invigorating, taking me from books and theory to the silt and gravel of real life in the city, from places classically associated with insiders to a world where outsiders were everywhere. This is where struggling, fragmented, mistake-making humanity washed up together and we tried to fumble our way through life, some with faith, some without, but all hoping that, next year, life would be recycled into something better. And Jesus demonstrated in his ministry that the real insiders were these very people who the world sees as outsiders: 'Many who are first will be last, and the last will be first' (Matthew 19.30). He made a beeline for those on the edge, society's outcasts, and thrilled them with the good news of the upside-down kingdom of God.

Mr Nixon was my hero. He was proud of having spent most of his life working on the canals – of which there are more in Birmingham than in Venice. He hadn't always been lucky and he'd lived for two years under a bridge on one of the canals. He'd ended up in an outhouse of the large rectory in which my wife and I lived in a flat up 48 stairs, and his single room had a bed without a mattress (his choice), a ring for cooking, and a small electric fire. At Christmas the government had started giving a winter fuel allowance, and each year Mr Nixon would come and find me and give me his allowance. He said he wanted me to 'give it to someone who really needs it'. This from a man who lived in an outhouse. Mr Nixon understood the message of Christmas. It's the feast of the outsider.

## As God is radically with us, so we need to be radically with others

I wrote earlier about the birth of Jesus as God being 'with' us at the most fundamental and committed level. God would be with us to the end, and beyond. That word 'with' is very important; it's at the heart of the gospel. This was no meet-and-greet visit with a chauffeur in the car and the engine still running. And it's our commitment to be with others that's one of our most distinctive responses to the incarnation. In a sense, Jesus wasn't in a hurry. He stayed with the family in an undistinguished village in the Galilean hills for 30 years, content to learn about being a builder, a brother, a worshipper at the synagogue, a member of the community, and gradually discerning the unique nature of his call from God, with all its far-reaching implications. He stayed and waited for the right moment. Jesus was 'with' us for a long time before he did anything 'for' us.

Our response to God's gracious commitment to us has surely to be our commitment to be with our struggling neighbours with whom we paddle through the mud of life. Huge numbers of people have discovered that the structure of the world has been declared unsafe, and as children of the same loving God we have a responsibility to go and be with them in whatever way we reasonably can. But this isn't easy.

When you come out of the cave beneath the Church of the Nativity you're immediately plunged into a contested world.

The sacred space is itself the subject of ongoing disputes between the Greek Orthodox, Armenian and Roman Catholic churches, disputes that have been known to become scuffles requiring police intervention. Outside, the Palestinian economy is wrecked and a separation wall 24 feet high runs around the city, speaking loudly of enmity and distrust. From the Shepherds' Fields you look across to a huge Jewish settlement, built illegally in Palestinian territory. All of this reminds us of the God who stepped into the heart of a real world with real-time conflict, who 'pitched his tent' (the meaning of 'dwelt' in John 1.14) in the midst of human folly to bring peace, hope and beauty to the dark places of life. As God is with us, so we need to be with those others who suffer most.

When I was a vicar in Taunton, as at most vicarages, homeless men would regularly come to the door, asking for food and a bed for the night. Food was easy: sandwiches and a mug of tea cost little. What cost more was the issue of accommodation. Simply giving cash is known to be an ineffective answer to the needs presented at the vicarage door. We had a shed that acted as our church paper store, a gathering place for newspaper that could be recycled for charity or church funds. I often offered this highly dangerous venue to our homeless regulars. Some chose the church porch instead and I would often find myself climbing over them to get into church the next morning.

But what disturbed me all the time was the fact that there, upstairs in the vicarage, was a warm, comfortable spare room. I would have let any friend or parishioner stay here if needed, so what was so different, *in Christian terms*, about my decision with regard to these homeless people? Of course, there are many common-sense answers to that question when you have young daughters and an unknown stranger, but there are many cultures where honouring the stranger with hospitality is a given. It wasn't the common sense of my decision that I doubted; I was troubled by a deeper discomfort about the distinctions I made and the commitments I would offer to different people.

God came to be with his people, and to stay there until the end. I'm inspired by those who manage so much better than me to echo that commitment in the care they offer to those who are knee-deep in the mess of the world. There's the man who feeds a million children a day from a garden shed near Oban. Magnus MacFarlane-Barrow, a Roman Catholic, was a fish farmer on the west coast of Scotland and volunteered as a charity worker in the Bosnian war. He later visited Malawi and it was there that he spoke to the 14-year-old son of a woman dying of AIDS. When asked what his dreams were, the boy, Edward, said, 'To have enough food to eat and to go to school.'

That did it. Magnus then started the charity that has become Mary's Meals, which feeds that huge number of children in hundreds of schools across 12 countries. When children get a meal at school, enrolment increases immediately and academic performance improves. The charity still runs from the corrugated iron shed that was the children's play room when Magnus was a boy. As God came to be with us, so this charity is with a million children, to change their lives.

Anne-Marie Wilson was an HR consultant with a regular income and a comfortable life in the UK, but in 2005 she was volunteering in a refugee camp in West Darfur when a ten-year-old girl walked into her life. She had endured female genital mutilation (FGM) and then been raped and become pregnant. Anne-Marie was so outraged at this that she began an anti-FGM charity, now called 28 Too Many after the 28 mainly African countries in which FGM takes place at the rate of some three million girls a year. Anne-Marie is a Christian and supported by the Church Mission Society. She goes to faith leaders, archbishops, the Pope, imams, as well as political leaders, to lobby for change. She's unstoppable, she's committed, as God demonstrated his commitment to us in Bethlehem.

As God is with us, so we need to be with others.

## The birth of Jesus says that paradox and vulnerability are OK

This conviction is a bit different. It comes from peeking into a manger and seeing a baby God. Christians believe that this is the real thing. This baby God isn't God pretending to be human (that's called Docetism), nor is it a human being masquerading as God (that's called Arianism). This child is fully human and at the same time fully divine. Neither is compromised. It's true that the early Councils of the Church had to argue for 300 years to come to an understanding of Jesus having two natures in the one person, but it was finally settled at the Council of Chalcedon in AD 451.

So there we have it: a baby God. But that's no more paradoxical than a carpenter King, or a crucified Messiah. Paradox seems to be a feature of anything we say about the life of Jesus. The very idea of the eternal Word, the creative principle behind the universe, becoming flesh is extraordinary. But that's the way it is. That's the scandal. And that's quite liberating for us as we try to follow Jesus and bear witness to the mystery of God. Why? Because it makes us realize that some questions can't be answered by Google. And in particular, it makes us enlarge our understanding of God.

Our common human tendency is to reduce the idea of God to a manageable size. Otherwise the concept of God gets out of control and slips out of our grasp like a giant octopus. So we like to keep things neat and tidy. God is this, not that. God approves of this, not that. God does this, not that. The idea of a baby God, however, blows that strategy out of our hands. God is this *and* that. God is here *and* there. God loves these people *and* those people (actually every person). We can no longer tie God down, possess God, tell God what he ought to think. It's often said that the opposite of one great truth may well be another great truth. It's only our limited minds and hearts that can't cope with paradox. Reality is not flat but deep, and welcoming paradox into our vocabulary is a sign that, for us, God is getting bigger and more sensational.

This understanding of Jesus as fully human – as well as fully divine – also gives us space to be vulnerable in our living and witnessing as Christians. One of the Christmas stamps a few years ago had Mary wiping away dribble from Jesus' mouth. He may have been the eternal Word, but here was the Word who couldn't say a word, so vulnerable was he.

Tina Beattie, in her book *The New Atheists*, puts it this way:

Christian theologians have continued to project images of virile masculinity onto God in the language of omnipotence and omniscience, but at the heart of the Christian faith is a different story about God – a God of vulnerability, love and compassion, who surrenders all claims to divine power by becoming the child in Mary's womb and the tortured man on the cross.[1]

When the Word became flesh, nails were driven through it.

I sometimes feel we ought to balance our talk of an almighty God with an all-vulnerable God. Pastorally that can make much more sense in tragic situations where an omnipotent God is an obvious object of anger for people who at some level believe that God must have allowed the calamity to occur. An all-vulnerable God is one who gave up omnipotence in the loving act of creating a free, evolving universe, but who now shares with us the grief that inevitably results. The cross vividly demonstrates God's solidarity with us in the suffering that's part of our common experience.

Honesty and vulnerability with each other in the fellowship of the Church would also deepen our relationships and help us break free of the ubiquitous word 'fine'. You know how it works: 'How are you?' 'Fine. You?' 'Yes, fine, thanks'. And that word can cover everything from 'I've had an amazing week of sheer delight,' to 'I've just had the most appalling week of my life.' I'd like to be able to issue on-the-spot penalties for overuse of the word 'fine'. So often we find that if we've experienced sadnesses that have drilled holes in our heart, sharing our vulnerability can release untold generosity in the people of God.

The paradox and vulnerability of Jesus' birth give us space and permission to own and exhibit both those characteristics in our discipleship and ministry. And as a result we might grow into the true beauty of our lives.

## We are never alone

At the end of a retreat by Galilee I asked the group what would be their most treasured 'take-home' memories. One woman spoke up immediately. 'Sunday worship with the local Christians in Nazareth,' she said. The rest of the group agreed. Back home some time later she still felt the same. 'On Sunday morning in church I often find myself back with those lovely people in

Nazareth. They were so friendly and hospitable.' And of course, one of the reasons they are so hospitable is that they are deeply grateful to Christians coming from around the world to let them know they aren't forgotten. Christians now make up less than 2 per cent of the population of Israel/Palestine and they can feel very isolated. They are the living stones, set among the ancient stones of the Holy Land, and it's important that they know they are not alone.

So it is with all of us. We need to know that we are not alone. This is particularly the case when we're trudging through dark territory, unsure of what's going to happen to us. It's a universal human need to know that we are not alone. The child who wakes up in a thunderstorm doesn't need a parent to stop the thunder; she just needs the parent to be there with her. The anxious husband going to see the oncologist doesn't need his wife to stop the cancer; he just needs her to be there with him.

God's coming in Christ to share our life is the ultimate assurance that we are not alone. It's not that we were alone before and then God arrived in Jesus. It's just that we didn't realize how graced we were with the presence of God until Jesus showed us. God had been unseen, beyond the bend of time, and Jesus brought God home to us. Now we know that God is always with us, closer than we can imagine, if only we'll open ourselves to receive him.

And when things are at their worst it's especially important to know we are not alone. Julian of Norwich was a fourteenth-century mystic who had many wise things to say following the intense visions she had when she thought she was on her deathbed at the age of 31. She later offered this reassurance to anyone going through times that drip with darkness like that: 'God did not say, "You shall not be tempest-tossed, you shall not be work-weary, you shall not be discomforted." But he did say, "You shall not be overcome."'[2] We will not be overcome because God never leaves us, and the nature of that presence is love – love that doesn't necessarily fix the problem but almost inevitably changes the experience.

The reason for this is that not only does God share our life, but then God changes it. We are never left as we were. We can't be touched by love without coming to life in some way or other. Indeed, the central invitation of the Christian gospel is to allow ourselves to be touched by that love and led into newness. Moreover, it isn't that we need to be good to find God, but rather that God finds us first with his dazzling love, and that leads us on to the path of being good. Or at least a bit better. 'We love because he first loved us' (1 John 4.19).

We are never alone. That's the promise. God said, 'I give you my Word.'

## Jesus grew up, and so must we

The nostalgia industry that our present-day Christmas has become puts Jesus in a manger, and wants him to stay there until next Christmas. We put the Christmas decorations away in the loft, secure in the knowledge that Jesus will still be there, safely tucked up, when we come for him next year. The trouble is, Jesus grew up.

You can see why society prefers to hang on to the baby. In the Christmas story we have all the ingredients necessary for a delightful nativity play with fluffy sheep, an unusual star, non-smelly shepherds, a bunch of wise men, some bemused cattle and, of course, the winning entry, a newborn baby. Later life proved somewhat rougher for Jesus. The child grew up to be a controversial teacher, setting both religious authorities and Roman rulers on edge. He taught a radical reworking of established religious practices, and backed that up with compassionate healings, over-the-top forgiveness, and an uncompromising solidarity with the oppressed underclass. He was bound to come to a bad end, and things came to a head one Passover in Jerusalem when the powers-that-be combined to rid themselves of this irritating Galilean preacher. They strung him up with conventional cruelty that involved whipping, random beatings, a crown of thorns rammed on his head, heavy-duty nails for hands and ankles, a blood-soaked cross, a final thrust from a well-used spear, and then burial of the destroyed body.

Not quite like Christmas.

So people say, 'Let's keep Jesus in a manger.' He'll be safe there, and so will we. But Christians are committed to the whole story, from the beauty of the birth to the nightmare of the cross. We want to point out the connection, the point of the story, what God was doing in all of this. We want to let Jesus grow up.

But if that's to be the case then we have to grow up too. Our faith starts off with the need to build some certainties, to put some scaffolding around our beliefs as we work out what makes sense to us. And that might involve choosing one way of thinking and not another, an either/or position. It probably involves reinforcing our views with the right preachers and priests. It almost certainly involves being in a church of like-minded people. Quite understandably, we're wanting to get a good, clear map of the faith so that we can find our way in new territory.

The problem is that if we get stuck in this stage of faith we can become both defensive and aggressive when people take a different view. We have to defend our hard-won way of believing or expressing our faith: a particular approach to the atonement, for example, or what happens to the bread and wine in the Eucharist. Or even prayer. When I went to teach in a theological college I remember being corrected by some students who thought my teaching and practice of prayer was deficient, since you could only pray if you knew Jesus as Lord and I had clearly suggested prayer might be a natural human response to life's many issues, which we can then develop into a mature prayer life. An early stage of faith can lead us to label, box and guard our beliefs to keep them pure.

There's nothing wrong with this need. It gives shape to our understanding of faith and helps us to make sense of the mystical jigsaw. However, if we remain forever in that place we'll be keeping Jesus in the manger. An honest faith will at some stage hit complexity. It won't answer all life's questions. It won't cope with some tragedy or trauma. It will be rocked by the convictions of someone we greatly admire but who sees things very differently. God is more elusive and doesn't seem to come at our beck and call. Our earlier certainties will begin to slip and need to be shored up by shouting louder.

It's then that either we lose the plot and drift away from faith, or we let Jesus grow up. Jesus went from the security of childhood and young adulthood in Nazareth into the open space of a public ministry, and eventually into the firestorm of Jerusalem in Holy Week. He needed more than a first-stage faith, important as that had been for Jesus as a devout child in Nazareth. He needed a faith that could face rejection, humiliation, torture and death at the hands of the Roman killing machine. We catch a glimpse of it in Gethsemane and on the cross: a faith made up of trust when his Father seemed to vanish, of love and forgiveness when he was stretched naked before every passing stranger, and of humble surrender when life was slipping away from him.

Jesus grew up and so, I contend, must we if we are to serve a world as complex, dangerous and bewildered as ours.

# 5

## *The killing: what happened?*

I could hardly believe it. It was my first time in the Church of the Holy Sepulchre, where the most serious event in the whole story of Christianity had occurred, and there was mayhem in every direction. We were swiftly ushered up the steep stone steps that led to the traditional site of the cross itself. Inevitably there were two chapels, one Roman Catholic and one Greek Orthodox. On this occasion the Greeks won. The crowds jostled their way towards the front and the opportunity to kiss the spot where the cross might have been planted. When I got there I hoped for a moment of calm in the chaos to reflect on the mammoth event itself, but the noise and chatter behind me made me conscious of hordes of other pilgrims waiting with varying degrees of patience, and the experience flashed by.

Down another set of steep stone steps and there was the spot reputed to be where Jesus was laid out in death. Pilgrims were kissing the stone reverently and wiping their scarves on it. I made my way through the crowds, having lost the company of all the rest of my group, and within 30 yards of Calvary there was the shrine itself, the Holy Sepulchre, the site of resurrection. Scaffolding surrounded the cube-like structure (though it has now gone), light streamed in from above, and a queue wound its way towards the entrance of the tomb, but all sense of the shape of the great church and all feelings of holy awe seemed unattainable. I was chiefly bent on survival.

But behind the chaotic scenes around the shrine I spotted a cave, quiet and welcoming, and then a cave within a cave, dark and unspoilt. It was a Syrian chapel in a first-century tomb and much more atmospheric than what was going on outside. I peered into the furthest cave and whispered the words, 'He is not here. He has risen.'

A few minutes later I was outside in the courtyard and I breathed calmly again. What had I experienced? This place represented the centrepiece of my faith. I was in awe of it, but confused. I needed time to process what I'd seen and felt. But through it all, I knew I had touched rock. This was where, by strong tradition, the death and resurrection of Jesus had taken place. It was from this point that the message of a new world of possibilities had ricocheted around the world.

But the journey Jesus took to this hallowed place had started five days earlier when he arrived at Bethphage on what we now call Palm Sunday. Presumably Jesus had spent the night with his friends Mary, Martha and Lazarus at Bethany, but next day he walked the short distance to Bethphage at the back of the Mount of Olives. There he sent two of his disciples to fetch the donkey that he'd arranged would be ready for him as he made his calculated entry into Jerusalem. Calculated because he was evoking the messianic hope of the prophet Zechariah, coming to the royal city riding on a humble donkey – not on a war horse as conventionally expected.

This was a clear challenge to both the religious and the imperial authorities. Jesus had come to bring the message of the kingdom to the heart of power, to see what the authorities would do with it, what they would do with *him*. This was where the message and the Messiah belonged, in Zion, the Holy City, but it meant coming face to face with a perfect storm of political, religious and economic power-brokers. The result, we know now, would be an ugly, miserable stitch-up.

The walk down the Mount of Olives is full of poignant interest. You pass the Pater Noster Church which celebrates the Lord's Prayer in scores of different languages. I generally ask people to say the prayer in any language they know other than their native one, and once had someone say it in sign language. You then descend the steep slope, keeping an eye on the sweep of Jewish stone tombs on your left, arriving in a few minutes at Dominus Flevit, the tiny church that reminds pilgrims of Jesus weeping over Jerusalem when he foresaw the city's destruction. The view from the terrace there is breathtaking, encompassing David's old city of Zion, the great sixteenth-century city walls, the Temple Mount with the astonishing golden Dome of the Rock, and many of the significant churches in Jerusalem. If Jesus paused here on his way down the Mount of Olives he would have seen the splendour and the corruption of the city laid out before him. He might also have seen his own destiny.

Further down you come to Gethsemane, and you're taken into the heart of darkness, where five days later Jesus handed over his life to frightened men to do their worst.

At that time Jerusalem was a city of about 30,000 people, but when Passover came round the population would have swelled to perhaps around 180,000. Pilate came too, from his usual home in Caesarea by the Mediterranean. He came up to this noisy, sweaty, emotional city only when he had to, but festivals were such times, when Roman power had to be on show, and crowd control was a priority. Jerusalem was seething, and to those anxious about their place in the jigsaw of power, it was dangerous. They needed everything to remain calm, without any upstart Galilean ratcheting up the emotional temperature. The religious authorities were already out to get him, and Judas' timely offer of betrayal was perfect.

Thursday night is when the meltdown began. On Sunday Jesus had come down from his donkey-ride into Jerusalem and gone straight into the Temple where he created an uproar, attacking the whole sacrificial industry, turning over the tables that changed local money into Temple coinage, and releasing the poor sheep, cattle and doves waiting patiently to be sacrificed. It was another calculated prophetic statement and certain to upset the authorities.

The week was spent in teaching the crowds, hungry for the vivid preaching that went deep into their souls, while the evenings were spent either with Mary and Martha or at supper with locals like Simon the leper, who was intrigued by this preacher who showed the likes of him such sympathy. But Thursday was coming.

The Synoptic Gospels – Matthew, Mark and Luke – locate the Last Supper and all that followed as a Passover meal, though John has it a day earlier. Either way, this is the meal on which men and women have meditated for centuries. In the Synoptics we have the template for the Eucharist and the prediction of Peter's denial. In John's Gospel we have the washing of the disciples' feet, the profound teaching of John 13—17, and Jesus' brief exchange with Judas before the betrayer slips out, ending with John's evocative phrase, 'And it was night' (John 13.30). In more ways than one.

A silent procession set off down the Kidron valley towards the garden of Gethsemane which Jesus already knew well (John 18.2). The meal had become progressively quieter as the disciples realized something very significant was going on, and when they left they were deep in thought. Gethsemane today is an enclosed garden with no more than 20 ancient olive trees alongside the ever-crowded Church of All Nations, this building housing a large expanse of rock on which, by tradition, Jesus bared his soul to his Father. Why is it that I always find I want to touch that rock? Pilgrims are looking for a connection, and ancient rock is as tactile a connection as one can get. Bread and wine, water and a towel, rock, and soon a kiss – this is a very tactile night. Jesus and the sleepy disciples would have heard on the still night air the tramp of boots and the chink of armour as the soldiers came down from the city, led by Judas, to claim their prize. There was a brief altercation, Jesus was seized, and the disciples fled.

I stood on the terrace of the church of St Peter in Gallicantu (meaning 'cockcrow') and looked down at the ancient steps leading up from the Kidron valley. This is one of those places in Israel where you know you've hit the spot. This was the way Jesus must have been brought from Gethsemane to the house of Caiaphas the High Priest for the series of encounters, beatings, trials and general confusion that surrounded Jesus before he went to meet Pilate. It was where, according to Mark, Caiaphas finally obtained what he had been hoping for: an admission by Jesus that he was indeed the Messiah (Mark 14.61–62; or Matthew 26.64: 'Tell us if you are the Messiah, the Son of God.' 'You have said so.'). Blasphemy! It just remained to get Jesus before Pilate as quickly as possible because only the Romans could impose the death penalty.

It would be good to be able to say that this church of St Peter in Gallicantu with its wonderful chapels and reverent atmosphere was the most likely site of Caiaphas' house, but many scholars think it's more likely that Caiaphas would have lived further up the hill where the smart houses were, next to what is now the Dormition Abbey. But there's a deep cell at Gallicantu with several Byzantine crosses traced into the opening, so there has certainly been a venerable history of belief that this is Jesus' cell. Whichever is true, St Peter in Gallicantu is at the very least close to where the savage show trial took place, and where Peter had his own hour of reckoning by a charcoal fire. As we sat in the silent chapel I pondered Peter's denial, imagining him trying to be as anonymous as a large, rough, northern fisherman could be in such circumstances. I pondered my many denials too.

There is what looks like a deep cell in the bowels of the church, without any redeeming features. It's stark and full of despair. With an unsuspecting pilgrim group corralled down there, I usually read Psalm 88 from up above, a voice declaiming,

> I am counted among those who go down to the Pit; I am like those who have no help, like those forsaken among the dead . . . You have put me in the depths of the Pit, in the regions dark and deep.

It's the aloneness of Jesus that gets me. Everyone has gone. The epitome of love, the joy of all the earth, the Lord of the eternal dance, has been utterly deserted. We come out quietly.

Jesus was then dragged to one of two places, either over to the former palace of Herod the Great at the Citadel by the Jaffa Gate, or across town to the Antonia Fortress where Pilate had his garrison. Popular devotion favours the latter and it's the place where we encounter the *lithostrotos* or pavement where John says that Pilate and Jesus passed judgement on each other in their famous debate about who Jesus was, where authority really lay, and 'What is truth?' (John 18.38). Pilate was uneasy at ordering the crucifixion of this impressive, enigmatic man, though he was seriously rattled by the possibility that he was claiming to be a king, and therefore a threat to Roman rule. He tried the ruse of releasing either Jesus or the notorious Barabbas, as it was the custom to release some prisoner or other at the festival, but the crowd had been whipped up to shout for Barabbas. Pilate gave up. He washed his hands of guilt, thus assuring himself a place in infamy, and released Jesus for the regulation beating, some special mockery involving a crown of thorns, and the dreadful punishment of crucifixion. Justice had been trampled underfoot but as far as the religious authorities were concerned vengeance had been meted out on this trouble-some Galilean preacher who dared to criticize the religious practices of the elite.

Then begins one of the most poignant journeys in the world. You might start in the Ecce Homo Convent of the Sisters of Zion who hospitably allow a Eucharist in their magnificent church, though some groups start a little further back at the Chapel of the Flagellation. In the Convent version you descend to what might have been the Roman pavement on which the confrontation with Pilate took place, noting the scratch marks of the soldiers' game 'King', after which you emerge on to the Via Dolorosa for the procession to begin. The moving thing about following this route, stopping and praying at each of the 14 stations, is how similar it is to what must have been going on when Jesus took this or a similar path, struggling with his terrible cross on his way to the hill called Golgotha ('place of the skull'). Crowds push and shove, tradesmen cajole potential customers, people shout noisy greetings to friends, men carry trays of food and drink with enviable dexterity, everything goes on as normal. You gather together under an easily missed plaque and read from the Scriptures, hoping your group can hear. You offer a loud prayer as if it's God who might not hear, then on you trudge, wending your way through the unforgiving throng of people.

So it must have been for that lonely figure, carrying the crossbeam of his own (imposed) weapon of self-destruction. Just another poor wretch, on his way to an agonizing death, but for Christians, the Saviour of the world on his way to a dreadful victory. It's a disturbing journey, relieved by a quiet passage over Ethiopian roofs and through a dark Coptic chapel, and then into the final stations in the Church of the Holy Sepulchre. We finish near the sepulchre itself, reading 1 Corinthians 15 as a kind of fifteenth station, but the hard work has been done earlier on the way.

The vastly ornate Greek altar above the place of crucifixion seems utterly distant from the stark black cross set against a darkening sky that awful 'Good' Friday. What happened here is beyond description, available only to the imagination. Here was a man, the cream of creation, reduced to silent suffering that we can't even grasp. To Christian eyes, here was God, naked in death as he had been naked in birth, submitting to humiliation. Jesus was hammered on to the crossbeam that he himself had been carrying, and then the cross was lifted up and dropped with an agonizing thud into its allotted hole, jarring his body from head to toe. Hideous pain shot through every bone and sinew. Then he had to settle into the terrible rhythm of raising himself on the nails so that he could get some air into his lungs to breathe, until he could stand the pain no longer and slumped down. Breathing then became desperately hard, so eventually he simply had to try and raise himself again on the nails. The murderous cycle continued until he had no more strength to push himself up, and he drowned in his own mucus. There are other details we don't need to explore.

The killing of Jesus is a story of horror and despair but also, strangely, of victory and transformation. Millions claim that it's the hinge on which the world turned. But how? How does one man's death 2,000 years ago change anything now? That's for the next chapter.

# 6

## *The killing: what does it mean?*

Many years ago, when we were still at university, my girlfriend and I went youth-hostelling in Switzerland. Unfortunately, my girlfriend had terrible earache which plagued her for days on end and nothing seemed to touch the pain. One morning, for some reason best known to my younger self, I chose to ask my suffering companion what she thought of the various theories of the atonement, and was surprised to receive a less than enthusiastic response. I can't remember her exact words but I was left in no doubt that the atonement was not up for discussion. I'm glad to say that I must have been forgiven because that girlfriend later became my wife.

The truth is that the atonement is never easy to discuss. What we see from afar is the glorious wreckage of the cross, and we know that something of supreme and ultimate importance was happening, but how to explain it? And yet we say that at 3 o'clock. on a Friday afternoon in Jerusalem nearly two thousand years ago God reconciled the world to himself. That's the scandal. Rowan Williams says of the disciples:

> They knew that because of the death of Jesus on the cross their universe had changed. They no longer lived in the same world. They expressed this with enormous force, talking about a new creation, about liberation from slavery. They talked about the transformation of their whole lives and they pinned it down to the events we remember each Good Friday.[1]

So as well as this 'scandal of particularity' there's something universal here too. The psychologist Carl Jung is supposed to have said that a naked man nailed to a cross is perhaps the deepest archetypal symbol in the Western psyche.[2]

Why is this catastrophic event so powerful? From the earliest days, followers of Jesus have tried to answer that question and nobody has got it right because the atonement isn't a problem to solve; it's a mystery to enter. Millions of us have gazed on that cross in wonder, knowing that something of vast importance was happening there, but knowing also that our limited categories of thought won't even come close to understanding the scale of this event. There's nothing neat and tidy about the cross, and to try to produce an all-embracing propositional theory of the atonement is a futile exercise.

People often say that Jesus came to die for us, but I think that's misleading. It suggests that Jesus had a death wish from the start, or that his Father was manipulating events so that Jesus would die in agony on a cross. Jesus didn't come to die for us; he came to live for us, to reveal the kingdom of God in all its fresh colours. Jesus came to demonstrate what the arrival of the kingdom meant, to open out the possibilities of a new world of grace, peace and justice, and to offer it to a jaded world. But what he found was that if you truly live like that in a world like ours, you run into a wall. In his case, a cross.

The crucial point, however, is that the mystery we have to enter and deepen is all about love. There are lots of other issues flying around, but the deep heart of what was happening is to do with love. At its simplest you could say that Jesus died of love. It was, of course, the Father's love that he embodied and expressed to the fullest extent possible in a human life. John says disarmingly that 'God is love' (1 John 4.8), so on the cross God in Christ was simply being what God is; what you see is what you get. Jesus was caught in the crossfire between love and hate, the love of the Father that he represented, and the hate of humankind that he was facing. He was caught in the open with nowhere to run, except to the Father's heart.

The cross, then, is about the ultimate mystery of love, a mystery that isn't open to inspection in a laboratory but is really only open to the receptive heart. Think of it as like the Koh-i-Noor diamond, which if you held it up would refract light in many colours from its various faces. The light striking the diamond is one; the reflections are many. All we can do with the cross, really, is hold it up to the light and see some of those reflections, those ways of comprehending the mystery. No approach is remotely sufficient by itself but together they give us some glimpses of what love did through that cross. The various approaches merge into the undifferentiated light of the love of God.

I found a bench a few yards away from that special altar in the Church of the Holy Sepulchre. People of all races and backgrounds were jostling for position. Hymns and chants were being sung; guides were giving commentaries; cameras were flashing; the hubbub was constant. And in all that confusion, and underneath the decorative flamboyance of the chapel, I tried to strip away the centuries and see a small hill outside the city walls, and in particular to see a gentle but determined prophet being hung out like so much refuse, dying by inches. Jesus was a pest to the Romans and a threat to the religious leadership, so they threw him on to the rubbish dump as they did all pests. Little did they realize that it was like trying to put out a fire with petrol. The whole world exploded.

## Love as substitute

As the writers of the New Testament struggled to understand that explosion, several images and metaphors emerged that cluster around the idea of Jesus being a substitute for humankind in facing the seriousness of the human condition. Jesus acting 'instead of' us.

Early one Sunday morning in Jerusalem I decided to make my way to the Holy Sepulchre in the hope of finding it quieter than it would be later in the day. I wandered along the empty *souk*, the narrow passage that had thronged with life the previous day. The sun slanted through the sturdy buildings, survivors of many centuries of commerce and violence. After a while I came across a man with a donkey cleaning up the previous day's copious quantities of litter. The donkey stood patiently on the stone passageway, laden with two large bags for the rubbish. Where the man and his donkey had already done their work the *souk* was clean, the stones shining where millions of feet had walked through the years. In front of the man and his donkey the previous day's rubbish was still strewn across the passageway, a mess of paper and foodstuffs and dust and grime. As I watched the patient creature taking ever more litter on to his back I couldn't help but think of the biblical image of the Lamb of God who takes away the sin of the world. Here it seemed to me was the donkey of God taking away the rubbish of the world. For a moment, time stood still.

There's a strong New Testament theme of Jesus taking away the sins of the world, doing something only he could do (John 1.29). The first generation of believers were quite clear that Jesus had suffered for us and had died for our sins. 'For I handed on to you as of first importance what I in turn had received: that Christ died for our sins in accordance with the scriptures' (1 Corinthians 15.3). Sometimes Jesus is seen as our representative (doing it for us), and sometimes he is seen as our substitute (doing it instead of us). But we have to treat the images they used with care.

The images come from several parts of the writers' social experience, such as the law courts, the marketplace and the Temple. They were not trying to formulate a definitive theory; they were doing their best to grasp an enormous event using the tools lying around in their culture. Paul, for example, was relentlessly scouring his experience for helpful metaphors, not to try to fix a doctrine in stone but to offer a glimpse of what was going on behind the terrible beauty of the cross.

The setting of the *law court* suggested the approach that humankind stands guilty before God of making an appalling mess of the world. Human sinfulness is both personal and corporate and the evidence against us is overwhelming. But instead of us facing the heavenly court and paying the penalty, Jesus in his love pays it for us. 'There was no other good enough to pay the price of sin; he only could unlock the gate of heaven and let us in.'

The setting of the *marketplace* allowed Paul to use the idea that we are like slaves held by an evil master, and Jesus paid the price to redeem us from slavery, to buy us our freedom. 'The Son of Man came . . . to give his life a ransom for many' (Mark 10.45).

The setting of the *Temple* picked up the rich theme of sacrifice and was used by both Paul and the writer to the Hebrews. In the Old Testament, giving an animal as a sacrifice covered over the sins of the person making the sacrifice (Leviticus 17.11), but already there was a growing sense that the real meaning of sacrifice was that it re-established the covenant between God and God's people, and that the heart of it was therefore to do with relationship and obedience rather than death itself.

> With what shall I come before the LORD? Shall I come before him with burnt-offerings, with calves a year old? . . . He has told you . . . what is good; and what does the LORD require of you but to do justice, and to love kindness, and to walk humbly with your God? (Micah 6.6–8)

On the cross, then, Jesus has acted in our place and offered God his perfect obedience, once for all, and therefore ended the need for continual sacrifices.

The strength of all these images, taken from the law court, the slave market and the Temple, is that they take the mess of humankind seriously. There's no value in God simply saying about our propensity for violence, cruelty, sexual abuse, genocide, exploitation: 'Oh, never mind, let's still be friends.' God would not be loving, just and good if God ignored the incredible inhumanities visited on so many people every day. Those inhumanities matter and must be dealt with. There is massive, objective wrong in the world that no just God can dismiss with easy forgiveness and a wave of the hand. When we hear on the news of rape as a weapon of war, of beheadings, of shells with chemical warheads, and of massive corruption at the expense of the poor, we must and should be angry. Evil must be confronted and dealt with. The substitutionary approach to the cross says that God did confront and deal with it, with love and through Christ.

But there are great dangers in letting these metaphors harden up into definitive 'theories of the atonement'. At its most banal it could seem as if people were so incorrigibly bad, and God was so deeply angry with them, that he would only forgive them if someone big enough could take the rap for the whole lot of them. So you have an angry God upstairs and a loving Jesus downstairs, with God demanding the blood of Jesus as punishment and payment. Sadly, I've encountered some awful illustrations that end up suggesting just this. But what is this saying about the God who is love? That an abstract idea of just-ice has a higher value than love and has to be appeased? And what is it saying about violence? That violence can save us? Violence can never be redemptive; it doesn't ever save, it destroys.

The key to hold on to with this substitutionary approach to the cross is that 'God was in Christ reconciling the world to him-self'(2 Corinthians 5.19, RSV). We must never separate the Father and the Son. God doesn't condemn Jesus, God condemns sin, which Jesus takes upon himself. God was not so *angry* with the world that he gave his only son, rather 'God so *loved* the world that he gave his only Son' (John 3.16). Love is always the key to any understanding of the cross.

We once had a drain outside our house that easily filled with disgusting debris and we had to put a gloved hand into the mess to pull out the gunge that was causing the blockage. If asked, I wouldn't have said that *my hand* was clearing out the drain; I would have said that *I* was clearing out the drain. It would have been futile to say, 'Poor hand, what a nasty job you have to do.' It was me doing it (or more likely, my wife). So Jesus wasn't sep-arated from his Father on the cross, taking God's punishment; 'God was in Christ reconciling the world to himself.'

The motivation of God in rescuing us from ourselves is always love.

## Love as example

There are some hymns that go straight to the heart every time you sing them. For me, one of the most affecting is Isaac Watts' 'When I survey the wondrous cross'. When I worked at Canterbury Cathedral, on Good Friday we would process from the area known as the Quire into the silent nave and there gather around a huge cross set up in splendid isolation. The great spaces of the cathedral echoed with silent grief. And there, looking up at this stark, majestic cross, we would sing:

> See from his head, his hands, his feet,
> sorrow and love flow mingling down:
> did e'er such love and sorrow meet,
> or thorns compose so rich a crown?

Were the whole realm of nature mine,
that were an offering far too small;
love so amazing, so divine,
demands my soul, my life, my all.

Absolutely. How can we resist such love? The New Testament is clear that Jesus died for love of us. 'God proves his love for us in that while we were still sinners Christ died for us' (Romans 5.8). It was a love that was defenceless but immense. The cross was the place where God demonstrated how totally he identified with the victims of the world, but also how far he would go to forgive even those who perpetrated such crimes upon those victims. 'Father, forgive them; for they do not know what they are doing' (Luke 23.34). Those who suffer and those who cause that suffering are all embraced in the love of God. This is a love that will stop at nothing. Don't we all want to be part of that, both receiving and passing on that love?

There's a striking contrast between what we do for love and what God does for love. What we do so often involves a love that's possessive, idolizing and sometimes aggressive. What God does involves the death of the young Prince of Life. Ultimately we believe that this love is irresistible because it's inexhaustible; it never gives up. 'Love is patient; love is kind; love is not envious or boastful or arrogant or rude . . . It bears all things, believes all things, hopes all things, endures all things' (1 Corinthians 13. 4, 7). I have rarely been reclaimed from my addiction to myself by a mighty act of God, but I have sometimes been able to turn away from that selfishness because I have caught sight of the crucified Christ, his face burning with love for me and for the world. That's what defeats me.

This powerful aspect of the cross was developed by the twelfth-century philosopher and theologian Peter Abelard. In a historical novel by Helen Waddell, he watches a rabbit die in anguish and sees there an image of God endlessly suffering the pain of the world. The cross is then the one moment when we see what God always suffers. Abelard says, 'O God, if it were true . . . it would bring back the whole world.'[3] Such love would be irresistible.

An equally powerful modern presentation of this theme is found in *Silence* by the great Japanese author Shusaku Endo, a book that has recently been made into a film by Martin Scorsese. It's set in the 1640s and is about an idealistic Roman Catholic priest, Father Rodrigues, who sets out with a companion from Portugal determined to help the brutally oppressed Japanese Christians, and to find his revered former teacher Father Ferreira, who's rumoured to have apostatized, renouncing his faith.

Finally the two meet. Father Rodrigues has been captured. He's not been tortured but he's mentally and physically exhausted. His captors tell him he must apostatize to save other captured local Christians from the horrendous torture and death known as the pit, and Ferreira comes to encourage him to do what he himself had done some years before. All Father Rodrigues has to do is walk on the face of Christ painted on a piece of wood called a *fumie*. That will be the sign of him renouncing his faith. Ferreira says:

'If you say that you will apostatize, those people will be taken out of the pit. They will be saved from suffering. And you refuse to do so? It's because you dread to betray the Church. You dread to be the dregs of the Church, like me . . . Yet I was the same as you. On that cold, black night I too was as you are now. And yet, is your way of acting, love? A priest ought to live in imitation of Christ. If Christ were here . . . Christ would have apostatized for them.'

'No, no!' said Rodrigues, covering his face with his hands and wrenching his voice through his fingers. 'No, no!'

Ferreira said, 'For love, Christ would have apostatized. Even if it meant giving up everything he had.'

'Stop tormenting me! Go away, away!' shouted the priest.

'You are now going to perform the most painful act of love that has ever been performed,' said Ferreira, taking the priest gently by the shoulder.

The priest raises his foot. In it he feels a dull, heavy pain. This is no mere formality. He will now trample on what he has considered the most beautiful thing in his life, on what he has believed most pure, on what is filled with the ideals and the dreams of man. How his foot aches! And then the Christ speaks to the priest. 'Trample, trample! I more than anyone know of the pain in your foot. Trample! It was to be trampled on by men that I was born into the world. It was to share men's pain that I carried my cross.'

The priest placed his foot on the fumie.[4]

It's a relentlessly demanding book and a very tough film to watch, but the themes it explores are central to the cross. 'You are now going to perform the most painful act of love that has ever been performed.' That's it; that's the cross, where Jesus is utterly demeaned, trampled on by men, in order to perform the most painful act of love that has ever been performed. Both trampled on and trampler. He identified so much with the sin and suffering of humankind, out of love, that he was prepared even to lose contact with God and go over the edge into death.

The strength of this image of the cross as demonstrating the love of God that is both vulnerable and inexhaustible is that it evokes a deep response in us, making us want to live for that love, and with that love empowering our own lives and actions. The weakness is that this response is subjective and it could appear that nothing objective has changed in the real world that Christ came to save. The horrors go on. Some of us might be changed inwardly but the world looks pretty much as it did before.

And yet this understanding of the cross has enormous power. In the words of another well-known hymn:

> Here might I stay and sing,
> no story so divine;
> never was love, dear King,
> never was grief like thine.
> This is my friend
> in whose sweet praise
> I all my days could gladly spend.

It's some such set of feelings that, year after year, has drawn me to my knees.

## Love as victor

There's another theme about the cross buried in the New Testament that doesn't get a huge amount of attention, but when it's apprehended seems to make sense to a lot of people. It's the theme of victory. The cross is the place where God took on the powers of evil and destruction, and won the strangest victory. Jesus was sucked into the darkness and although it broke him, it also broke itself. Sin was defeated; death died. It's an understanding of the cross that was embraced by the early Fathers of the Church and then picked up again in the twentieth century by the Swedish theologian Gustaf Aulén in his influential book *Christus Victor*.[5] You can see the theme in the sixth-century hymn by Bishop Venantius, 'Sing, my tongue, the glorious battle, sing the ending of the fray,' or the much later hymn, 'The strife is o'er, the battle done, now is the Victor's triumph won.'

Perhaps the key phrase is the one quoted by John as the last word of Jesus from the cross where he says, 'It is finished.' Mark's Gospel just says he gave a loud cry, but John tells us what that cry was: '*Tetelestai*' – 'Done it!' (John 19.30). Jesus had confronted everything that a wild world could throw at him. He had drunk the last dregs of evil, taking away all the dark toxicity left in the bitter cup. Jesus had warned his friends at his last meal with them: 'In the world you face persecution. But take courage; I have conquered the world!' (John 16.33). Even earlier, when warning them about his approaching crisis, he had used similar imagery: 'Now the ruler of this world will be driven out. And I, when I am lifted up . . . will draw all people to myself' (John 12.31–32). The language of victory is picked up in the letters of Paul and the early Church: 'He disarmed the rulers and authorities and made a public example of them, triumphing over them' (Colossians 2.15).

The trouble with some of this language, of course, is that it can seem to be somewhat abstruse and the image of principalities and powers doesn't sit easily with many contemporary world-views. Let's see if we can demystify this a bit. For one thing, the victory of Jesus was the victory that he had been winning all through his ministry. All along, Jesus had been offering a life of love and obedience to his Father. The fruits of that life had been there for all to see: 'The blind receive their sight, the lame walk, the lepers are cleansed, the deaf hear, the dead are raised, and the poor have good news brought to them' (Matthew 11.5). The victories were already apparent, for those who could see.

In the Apostles' Creed we speak of Jesus as 'born of the virgin Mary, suffered under Pontius Pilate', but hidden there is, of course, the 'Christ of the comma' who fits in between those two phrases. The whole life of Jesus lies unspoken, represented only by that comma. But in that life is the continual victory of love as Jesus preaches, heals, convinces and inspires, confronts hypocrisy and falsity, and takes the side of the poor. It's that victory that is finalized on the cross.

It's also possible to break down the metaphysical language of evil and conflict into some quite visible elements of life in that time and culture. Many powerful forces met the powerlessness of Jesus on the cross, but Jesus' 'powerlessness' was indestructible. Jesus was confronting physical power in the hands of the soldiers, political power in the hands of a cruel imperial governor, religious power in the hands of an established elite with much to lose, cultural power in the shape of a well-tuned system framed around the sabbath and the Temple, economic power shared out by the wealthy deal-makers, and spiritual power that was and is always present in the manipulations of men and women. So Jesus stood against all these powerful forces and refused to accept their authority. He entered their world and disarmed them by remaining true to himself, to his Father and to the way of love. He wouldn't curse God and die. He wouldn't blame his murderers. He wouldn't resort to anger, bitterness or even selfishness – his concern was for his mother and his friend (John 19.26–27), for the robber at his side (Luke 23.43), and for those who were abusing him. Jesus retained his integrity and his lifelong faithfulness to his Father. It was astonishing; nothing could penetrate the armour of love, so much so that the centurion and the soldiers overseeing this shoddy judicial murder are quoted by Matthew as saying, 'Truly this man was God's Son!' (Matthew 27.54).

I have one picture that comes to mind when I think of this approach to the cross. Many of us will have had a small child who sometimes got beside himself or herself with anger, and all you could do was embrace the child, absorb the blows, and wait until the little body flopped, all passion spent. You might have felt somewhat pummelled in the process but it was the only way for that little person to discharge his or her anger or frustration. Your task was simply to soak it up, to win by losing.

So the cross was God in Christ absorbing the world's mess and sin, and not giving it back. Jesus used no swords and shed no blood except his own. He simply overcame evil with good. That's the victory of love. He held the pain rather than pass it on to others. In Christ, God's love was tested to destruction, and still it held true. Spiritual writer Ronald Rolheiser puts it like this:

> Jesus took away the sin of the world by taking in hatred and giving back love; by taking in anger and giving out graciousness; by taking in envy and giving back blessing; by taking in bitterness and giving back warmth; by taking in pettiness and giving back compassion; by taking in chaos and giving back peace; and by taking in sin and giving back forgiveness.[6]

That's our task too.

## Love as participation in God's great story

There's just one other approach to the cross that either undermines or embraces all that has gone before, depending on your viewpoint. Even though I have tried to avoid calling the three previous approaches 'theories of the atonement' they might still seem somewhat propositional in nature. And propositions can seem abstract and not sufficiently connected with everyday life.

Instead we could start where the first Christians started, with their lived experience and the larger framework of God's story into which their own wonderful new experience of the risen Christ fitted. God's Big Story is essentially a love story, as God continues the search he started in the Garden with the evocative question, 'Adam, where are you?' The story of God's love for his people took in the often-renewed Covenant with God's people, the Passover and escape from Egypt, the various attempts to establish a faithful people in their own land, the Exile when they failed, and the hope of a Messiah to put things right. Enter Jesus, the faithful One, whose life of radical love and direct challenge took him to the cross, and beyond. And now the Church is pledged to continue the work of Jesus until the curtain is brought down and all things are gathered up in Christ (Ephesians 1.10).

So far so good. But what does that really mean for us? How do we fit into the Big Story today? The key lies in Paul's contention in Romans 6.3–4:

> Do you not know that all of us who have been baptized into Christ Jesus were baptized into his death? Therefore we have been buried with him by baptism into death, so that, just as Christ was raised from the dead by the glory of the Father, so we too might walk in newness of life.

The picture we get here is that we don't just observe the cross from afar, we *participate* in it. The atonement isn't just a proposition; it's a way of life. It's the way of discipleship, living in the cross through sacrificial loving of our neighbour day by day. The cross then becomes a pastoral imperative, not just a belief to file away under 'C'. I fit into God's Big Story as I participate in God's loving presence in and with the world, and in particular with the poor.

This leads Sam Wells to stress again the importance of the word 'with' that we encountered in Chapter 3. 'God with us' really *is* the gospel. 'Jesus is Immanuel before he is Saviour,' present *with* us before doing anything *for* us, and 'the notion of "at-one-ment" might therefore be reconfigured as "re-with-ment".'[7] Our isolation from God and one another is overcome by a God who is unconditionally *with* us and has demonstrated that commitment from the manger to the cross and beyond. Our calling is similarly to be unfailingly *with* our neighbour through the grace that flows from the cross.

As I sat on that bench in the Church of the Holy Sepulchre trying to strip away the distractions, it has to be said that I wasn't thinking of any of these different ways of understanding the cross. I was simply trying to be there, with Christ, and to identify with the terror of that day. I was imagining Mary, beside herself with grief, and John, helplessly crying inside as his friend suffered such agony. Above all, I was there with Jesus, the best that human life could be, and wondering again at the stupidity of humankind and the miracle of divine humility. It was for me a time of anguish and of grace.

> He came from his blest throne,
> salvation to bestow;
> but men made strange, and none
> the longed-for Christ would know.
> But O, my Friend,
> my Friend indeed,
> who at my need his life did spend.

# 7

## *The killing:*
## *what does it mean for us now?*

So we've looked at what happened that dark day in Jerusalem when the pain of the world funnelled down on to Jesus, and we've explored some of the different ways that men and women have tried to grasp just the edge of what it all meant, what was really going on. But where does that leave us, living today far removed from the event, the culture in which it took place, and the assumptions of Christendom that prevailed in the West for hundreds of years but are now melting away? Christians maintain that this event is the hinge of history, the pivot on which all life swings, but how do we get hold of such a momentous event and let it shape our lives?

When I step out of the Ecce Homo Convent in Jerusalem at the start of the Way of the Cross, the Via Dolorosa, I always feel both the significance and the insignificance of what we're doing on this stage of the pilgrimage. On the one hand we're about to retrace the steps of Jesus, a journey that could claim to be the most important one the world has ever known. On the other hand, I'm aware of how people in the street ignore us, bustling about with their various jobs, earnestly pursuing their various errands. How does our anonymous procession make any difference to the many worlds around us? Why are we doing this? But still, we walk on.

### The only way is love

I have maintained that Jesus died of love. He had lived to the end with the values on which his life was based, which were those of love, obedience to his Father and trust in God's wisdom. I have therefore framed the various approaches to the atonement in

61

terms of love – love as substitute, love as example, love as victor and love as participation in God's great story. It follows that the cross tells us, definitively, that the only way is love.

But I don't mean any of the fluffy, celebrity-magazine, fridge-magnet types of love. I mean a love that's as tough as nails. Jesus was a man of infinite compassion around a steel core. He was the man who didn't condemn the woman caught *in flagrante* with her lover; he was the man who spoke of forgiving seventy times seven times if the situation demanded it; he was the man who gave us the iconic figure of the prodigal son's father. There was no doubting his tenderness. But his pursuit of his mission was relentless. He 'set his face to go to Jerusalem' (Luke 9.51) and he never looked back, though he knew what it was bound to mean. He refused to compromise in his condemnation of religious cant and hypocrisy. He threw the money-sharks out of the Temple. He stiffened his resolve in Gethsemane. He turned down every opportunity to compromise at his trial. He kept on, one step after another, to the end.

The only way is love, whatever it costs. I need to believe that, and to live it, if I want to be transformed by the cross. And, rather pathetically, I do my best – but how compromised that is. It's easy to do the odd loving thing and feel good about it. It's less easy to make love a way of life. Most of us can do the set piece, but a life of genuine authenticity is more difficult. When Jesus talked about picking up your cross he wasn't meaning being patient when you have a headache. The cross is a way of love such that if you cut through us like a piece of seaside rock you would find the word 'love' printed right the way through us. But it can only happen if we live, daily, within the love of God. 'Abide in me as I abide in you' (John 15.4).

Love is a cup of coffee with a troubled friend; love is sending a card of encouragement; love is staying on to clear up after everyone else has gone home; love is remembering to phone; love is listening; love is giving to that disaster fund even though you're a bit short yourself; love is visiting even though she has dementia; love is volunteering at the holiday club; love is praying for the person you said you'd pray for. Love is for life, not just for Christmas.

## I don't have to earn my way into the kingdom

There's a persistent rumour that to get into God's good books you have to do lots of good things. Then when the books are opened at the end of life, and the ticks and crosses are added up, if we've got a reasonable score we're OK. I parody, but it's undeniable that deep down we often believe that we have to earn our right to God's favour. And the cross says, 'No, you don't need to do that.'

God doesn't love us because we're good. God loves us because *God* is good, and then we might become good our-selves because we can draw on the infinite Source of goodness that is God. That's such a relief. The cross is the sign and seal of God's goodness. It's what Christ did for us on that dark cross that matters, because that's where the mess we make of life, and that life makes of us, was cleared up. (The traditional lan-guage is that sin and death were overcome.) It was all done for us; so now we can walk in the freedom of the children of God.

Many people will remember the tragedy of the ferry *Herald of Free Enterprise,* which sank off Zeebrugge in 1987, and some will recall the many acts of heroism and self-sacrifice performed by ordinary people as they assumed responsibility for the lives of others. Four men on one of the lower decks took it in turns to hold the head of an elderly woman above water. A passenger with spinal injuries carried his baby daughter to safety with his teeth. One man used his body as a bridge to enable people to move to a safer part of the ship. These were wonderful actions, but the point I'm making is that the recipients of this heroism would have said, 'It was all done for us'; they didn't have to do anything but receive the benefits of those actions, and live.

It behoves us, then, to live as people who have been set free and given life through the action of Jesus on the cross. Someone on the doomed ferry said later, 'Perhaps we are more loving people, more sensitive, more concerned for each other because of that moment of grief which overthrew our ideas of what things matter, and opened our eyes again to the importance of our common humanity.'

The cross might teach us that goodness isn't necessary to earn God's love, but it's quite likely to be the result. Indeed, if it isn't the result it can't be said that God's love has truly penetrated our lives.

## The suffering God is always with us

For Jesus the cross was a personal disaster as well as an inevitable destiny. Those awful words he uttered, 'My God, my God, why have you forsaken me?' echo through history, and send a chill through every believer. For Jesus it was a death within a death because from the sixth hour he became an orphan. He had given his mother away to John for him to look after, and now it seemed that the Father had died on him too. He had lost both his parents. So those words of forsakenness sear our hearts.

And yet, his Father had not forsaken him. He was with him, as he always had been, but the way Jesus identified with our alienation from God was so complete that he experienced the loss that is normally ours. The deepest truth is that God is always present. God is simply not able to be absent from any part of his creation, particularly the darknesses.

In his moving book *One for Sorrow*, Alan Hargrave writes about the traumatic loss of his 21-year-old son. He says:

> That cross became very important for us. It is the cross of suffering and pain, I cannot even begin to think about resurrection. I cannot bear the thought of a glorious, victorious God in heaven, but I can just about bear the thought of a God who comes down to earth, who takes on human form, lives our life, grows up in the carpenter's shop, works in the family business, enjoys a drink with his mates, goes to weddings, becomes famous and popular for a while, then suffers rejection, betrayal by one of his closest friends, desertion and denial by the rest, a mock trial, flogging that rips the flesh off his back in chunks, and a cruel agonizing death, hanging, gasping for breath, on a cross. The God who knows what it's like to lose a son – an only son in his case. This is a God who knows what it's like to suffer. This is the only God I can relate to just now, in any shape or form.[1]

Geoffrey Studdert Kennedy was an army chaplain in the First World War. He was known as Woodbine Willie because he always had a supply of cigarettes to offer to the soldiers. It wasn't surprising that he struggled with the meaning and relevance of faith in the context of such terrible suffering. And he wrote this:

> On 17th June 1917 I was running to our lines half mad with fright through what had once been a wooded copse. It was being heavily shelled. As I ran I stumbled and fell over something. I stopped to see what it was. It was an undersized, underfed German boy with a wound in his stomach and a hole in his head. I remember muttering, 'You poor little devil, what had you got to do with it? Not much great blond Prussian about you.' Then came light. It may have been pure imagination but that doesn't mean it wasn't also reality. It seemed to me that the boy disappeared and in his place there lay Christ upon his cross, and he cried, 'Inasmuch as you have done it to the least of these my little ones you have done it to me.' From that moment on I never saw a battlefield as anything but a crucifix. From that moment on I have never seen *the world* as anything but a crucifix.[2]

The world a crucifix. It seems that reality often has a cruciform shape as people suffer in all manner of ways. The cross is a sign of the presence of Christ with us, always and everywhere, in a world both glorious and brutal. Our response can only be to stay close to the One who stays close to us. The arms of the cross are stretched out to hold us, whatever state we're in and whatever's happening to us. 'He opened wide his arms for us on the cross.'

Everybody has a breaking point – only God doesn't. That was the victory of the cross. Love couldn't be broken, and so it's to that love that we go, not for magic solutions, but for deep safety and for healing.

## We are released from our imprisonments

I never fail to be amazed at the ability of advertisers to trivialize anything. One of our major supermarkets had a slogan one Easter that said, 'Great offers on beer and cider: Good Friday just got better.' That the supermarket could claim that the momentous tragedy of Good Friday would get better with beer and cider almost defies belief.

What the advert displayed is society's inability to distinguish the serious from the trivial. Good Friday was about deeply serious matters, one of which was that it tackled our enslavements. An obsession isn't necessarily a bad thing. To be obsessed with cricket, for example, is clearly a sign of good judgement. But most of us would admit (confidentially, and in the right conditions) to being addicted to, or imprisoned by, habits and responses that are negative and harmful. The list is as long as your arm: pride, jealousy, self-righteousness, alcohol, stubbornness, gambling, greed, mental cruelty, arrogance, pornography, complaining, small-mindedness, gossip, a dismissive attitude to others, overbearing competitiveness and so on.

We're not going to rid ourselves of all traces of the habits that have usually been loved, preserved and fostered over many years, but the promise of the cross is that their power can be broken. Charles Wesley expressed it vividly in the hymn 'And can it be':

> Long my imprisoned spirit lay,
> fast bound in sin and nature's night;
> thine eye diffused a quick'ning ray,
> I woke, the dungeon flamed with light;
> my chains fell off, my heart was free;
> I rose, went forth and followed thee.

This has been the continual witness of countless Christians, even if there has to be a proper caution about rejoicing too soon or, in biblical terms, finding that seven evil spirits have returned to an empty house (Luke 11.26). The cross is the key to this freedom. This is where victory was won over all the negatives that assail us, all the obsessions and addictions that alienate us from God, ourselves and others. This is where once, for all, darkness was absorbed in the light and constancy of God. It's why we're invited in Ephesians to recognize that 'once you were darkness, but now in the Lord you are light. Live as children of light' (Ephesians 5.8).

I should have told the supermarket that there are more important things to enjoy than beer and cider.

## We have a compelling vocation to confront evil

One of the terrible beauties of the cross is that it calls a spade a spade. It doesn't dissemble; there's no spin. Evil is evil and on the cross it's in a fight-to-the-finish conflict with good. And of course, from the outside, and from God's perspective, things didn't look to have gone well. The worst that we could imagine had happened. The Word of God fell silent on Golgotha, and the earth shook with pain. The Trinity went into meltdown. That's how serious it was.

And that's how serious it is that evil is named and confronted wherever it appears in our world. There are times and places for compromise on lesser matters but on the clearest issues of good and evil there can be no equivocation. And so it's important to recognize that on the cross we don't see passive submission to evil but rather we see *the price Jesus paid for an active challenge to evil.* It's that active challenge that Christians are called to. And, to be clear, Christians may also find that they have to pay a high price when they confront evil. People profiting from dark deeds don't give up without a fight, and they may fight dirty. Theologian Herbert McCabe summarized Jesus' teaching like this: 'If you don't love, you're dead; and if you do, they'll kill you.'[3] Followers of a crucified Lord should know that there's no crown without thorns.

But it's good to see that in Christian history the challenge has been taken up time after time. Whether it's in confronting slavery, child labour, terrible prison conditions and awful factory practices in the nineteenth century; apartheid, urban decay, world poverty and the denial of human rights in the twentieth century; or human trafficking, social inequality and climate change in the twenty-first century, Christians have always been in the front line. Christian faith isn't for the complacent – though we need quiet prayer as much as energetic action. But for the Christian it's beyond doubt that social and political action are part of discipleship. Justice is the political form of compassion, the social form of love.

All this flows from the life and teaching of Jesus who put his life on the line for truth and justice, and paid the price. So do many Christians today. It's the visible form of taking up your cross.

## The new way is reconciliation

A man was staying with Elias Chacour, the Melkite Archbishop of Galilee. The visitor was explaining how hard he was finding it to love the Jews because of their attitude to the Palestinians. Elias Chacour said to him, 'For every Palestinian you love, you must find a Jew to love too. This is the only hope for our nation.' Many who have travelled to Israel/Palestine will know how demanding and wise that statement is.

Reconciliation is hard but it's at the heart of the gospel. Paul says, when writing about how being in Christ makes everything new:

> All this is from God, who reconciled us to himself through Christ, and has given us the ministry of reconciliation; that is, in Christ God was reconciling the world to himself, not counting their trespasses against them, and entrusting the message of reconciliation to us.     (2 Corinthians 5.18–19)

There are four references to reconciliation in those two verses.

There's one caveat to apply here. Forgiveness takes one person, but reconciliation takes two. It's often pointed out that through the cross not only were we reconciled to God but, in a sense, God was reconciled to us as well. Why so? Well, we never asked for a world as messed up as this; we were never consulted. Nevertheless, we have to manage the earth's capacity to kill and destroy, the body's tendency to break down and cause immense pain, and the dangerous freedom given to damaged people who damage others. So, in this way of thinking, God also needs forgiving for creating a world like this in the first place. Perhaps, then, this reconciliation runs both ways. The cross is the place where we meet.

Whichever way you look at the issue of reconciliation it's clear that it's a central theme of the cross, and if we are to live in the way of the cross we will have forgiveness and reconciliation as major imperatives. Unfortunately society is plagued by binary thinking. It's either/or, good or bad, in or out, true or false. Some people say, 'If I don't know who I'm against, how do I know who I am?' But this way disaster lies. A Chinese proverb says, 'Whoever opts for revenge should dig two graves.' We remain in our own prison if we're unable to forgive and be reconciled. Reconciliation sets both parties free, and forgiveness is the best route to reconciliation.

Of course, the tricky thing about forgiveness is that it has to be premature or it's not forgiveness. Jesus didn't say, 'Father forgive them – if they apologize.' Grace doesn't wait and see. It acts first, takes the risk, acts as if the relationship is already made good. That's very hard. Indeed, sometimes it proves impossible for people who have been terribly hurt and who, spiritually and emotionally, can't get to a place of forgiveness. Forgiveness is a process, or perhaps better, it's an attitude of hope; but it can't be demanded by another.

And yet, when forgiveness is possible, it's deeply liberating. It's the emotional equivalent of losing excess weight and feeling healthier and happier. Mark Oakley tells a remarkable story in his excellent book *The Splash of Words*:

> I was brought up by my grandparents. As a boy I knew that my grandfather had flown in the Royal Air Force in the Second World War and he was a bit of a hero to me but he never spoke about his experiences, except one day mentioning 'Dresden' and weeping. He has since died but a few years ago I was asked to preach in the reconstructed Frauenkirche in Dresden. He was very much in my mind. On the way to the railway station at the end of my visit the taxi driver asked me why I was in Dresden and I told him I had always wanted to come. 'Why?' he asked. I took a deep breath. 'Because my grandfather was a navigator of a Lancaster bomber and I know he flew here on 14 February 1945 as part of the bombing raid and he could never talk about it.' The man was quiet and then said, 'Ah, that was the night my mother was killed.' He pulled the car over and turned the engine off. He then turned round to me, put out his arm towards me and said, 'And now we shake hands.'[4]

As Martin Luther King said, 'We must live together as brothers (*sic*) or we perish together as fools.' And the reconciliation we so badly need flows from the cross where our sad divisions are overcome.

## We need to learn how to die

The deeper journey of faith isn't just about religious obser-
vance, it's about letting go of our lives so that God's life can
flow through them. That's roughly what Jesus meant by saying:

> If any want to become my followers, let them deny them-
> selves and take up their cross daily and follow me. For
> those who want to save their life will lose it, and those who
> lose their life for my sake will save it.     (Luke 9.23–24)

Let go, he says, and you'll find more than you ever dreamed
possible. But first we have to learn how to die to so much we
take for granted.

The Gospels show Jesus often talking about his approaching death. Three times he does this in Mark, and three times
the disciples change the subject. So eventually Jesus stopped
talking about it and just did it. He turned towards Jerusalem
and events unfolded as he had predicted. But Jesus usually
coupled predictions of his death with this call to the disciples
to take up their own cross and lose their lives too.

The problem for most of us is that, like the disciples, we
don't want to lose our lives, to give them up, hand them over.
We don't want to lose control of our lives (or, sadly, the control
that we often exercise over the lives of others). But until we've
learned to let go of our smaller self we won't be able to enter
the deep river of grace that flows beneath the surface of our
lives, and thereby discover our true self. The Franciscan writer
Richard Rohr calls this 'winning by losing'. But it's a kind of
dying, and so we resist it, thereby limiting ourselves to pad-
dling in the shallows of God's amazing grace. We often remain
consumers of religious activities rather than participants in the
deep flow of God's life.

The point is that the message of the cross and resurrection,
of death and new life, isn't just a theological motif; it's a pat-
tern that we see across life, throughout nature, and in common human experience. The natural world dies in winter and
is renewed in spring. Generations live, die and are replaced.
Organizations flourish for a while and are overtaken by newer,
faster operations. Civilizations seem immutable but they suffer

decay like the rest of us and are replaced by others. It's not surprising that initiation rites are always about death and new life.

And in the spiritual life, which sustains us in everything we are, it's important that we learn the way of descent, of letting go, rather than pinning our hopes and plans on a constant experience of ascent. When we let go (learn to die) we find that we are united with God in a way that is richer than ever, more peaceful, less plagued by effort and argument. We find God in all things. We aren't worried by uncertainty and paradox. We enjoy diversity and revel in the wideness of God's mercy. We feel as if we're carried along by the mystery and abundance of God.

There's a moving French film called *Of Gods and Men* which is based on true events that took place in 1997 when terrorists took over many mountain villages in Algeria. Eight Trappist monks were strongly encouraged by the authorities to leave their monastery but they decided to stay and continue their simple life of prayer and service alongside the villagers. They were taken hostage by the terrorists who demanded an exchange of prisoners with the French government, which of course wasn't playing. The last scene in the film is of the monks being taken off to what we know now is their death. They plod off in silence up the mountainside, gradually disappearing into the mist until we see them no more. Eventually the credits roll but the audience sits in silence.

At a deeper level it seems as if the lives of these monks are disappearing into Christ. They have handed their lives over, taken up their cross, and now martyrdom is about to complete their union with the One they have served with such devotion for so long. Their silent disappearance in the mist is a disappearance into endless life in God. There's nothing more to say, nothing more to ask for. We watch in silence.

Jesus, hanging on a cross, also disappeared into endless life in God, which we glimpse briefly, bathed in light and brushed with gold, in the resurrection appearances. Perhaps this is the chief meaning of the cross for us: that in letting go of our lives, in 'disappearing', we can know something of the beauty of resurrection.

# 8

## *The manhunt: what happened?*

I'm back at the cube-shaped tomb in the Church of the Holy Sepulchre. I'm in the queue winding slowly towards the entrance where two Greek Orthodox monks, with a minimum of niceties, usher pilgrims inside. I wonder why I'm doing this when the sepulchre feels so alien to the picture of the empty tomb I've always imagined from the Gospel accounts. But it feels as if I should do this at least once.

I get to the head of the shuffling queue and before I know it I'm being waved forward into an antechamber and then the main tomb, now a chapel with sparkling ornaments and burning tapers around the waist-high, pinkish-grey stone slab that now serves as an altar, but is revered as the stone on which Jesus had been laid in death. I hardly have time to look around and take it in, let alone reflect on the extraordinary event that happened here, before I'm being summoned out; my 30 seconds is up. I feel vaguely cheated, but whether it's from the shortage of time or the distinctly nineteenth-century feel of the tomb (repaired after a fire in 1808), I'm not sure. I need to sit and think.

Certainly this spot has good claims to authenticity. The site was known by the Jerusalem community even after Hadrian built a shrine to Aphrodite over it in AD 135. When Queen Helena arrived in the fourth century local Christians were still able to identify the site where Jesus had died and been buried. Helena's son Constantine had his engineers dig out the tomb so that it stood clear of the surrounding rock, and he covered it with a rotunda 40 metres wide as the focus of a five-nave basilica, dedicated in 335. A crypt at the far end of the church is the place where Helena made another of her discoveries, one which she said was the true cross itself. Pieces of that cross have rather improbably turned up in churches and shrines all over the world ever since.

The basilica was systematically destroyed in 1009 and the tomb was attacked with picks and hammers until it was effectively levelled. It was therefore the Crusaders who restored the church over the 50 years from 1099, and it's their church that we see today. This means that there isn't a definitive paper trail to the original site, but there is a stone trail and that's even better. I had been at the best authenticated site of the resurrection event that holds and grounds my faith.

But creep behind the sepulchre and you find a dark Syrian chapel, complete with decrepit furnishings and a battered altar. Usually it's blessedly quiet after the noise and bustle outside. Looking into a cave off the chapel you see a first-century Jewish burial chamber that must have been the innermost section of a catacomb where the body of Christ would have been laid. Now we're getting somewhere. This feels authentic. This is where I like to spend time in thought and prayer.

There's another lovely site to visit that commemorates the resurrection beautifully, if not historically. This is the place that General Gordon of Khartoum spoke of in 1883 as he looked out of a window and saw a small hill behind the present Old City bus station on which he made out the features of a skull (Golgotha, 'place of a skull'). Here he found a two-room, first-century tomb, which is now set in a tranquil garden and much visited by British pilgrims. It offers a restful place to pray and ponder with the help of a highly evocative visual example of a first-century tomb. If you can't imagine the women turning up here with their spices, or Peter and John skidding to a halt outside the tomb, you're not really trying.

Of course, belief in the resurrection is the touchstone of the Christian faith. No resurrection, no Christianity. I get genuinely excited by the resurrection but I have to admit it's hard to pin down. A four-year-old member of our family was trying to puzzle it all out. 'The bad people did kill him,' he said, 'but then he was alive, but then he was dead again, but then he was alive again. He was dead two times but he was alive four times.' It's confusing. And to some people it's clearly eccentric nonsense. Richard Dawkins has said of the resurrection, 'It's so petty, it's so trivial, it's so local, it's so earthbound, it's so unworthy of the universe.' There are many intelligent people who might just be able to travel with Christian believers in the power and importance of the cross, but who part company with Christians at the possibility of Christ returning to life some time after his well-attested death. Indeed, any thoughtful Christian has to have sympathy with that view, even if they disagree with it. Theologian David Ford wrote:

> There is no ready-made worldview into which [the resurrection] fits. As a God-sized event the same considerations apply to it as to the reality of God: if we think we have a framework that contains it, then we have not grasped the sort of event it is.[1]

So we're right outside our comfort zone here. In a sense we'd rather not have to handle the resurrection because it's too big; it explodes in our hands. On the other hand, it's the irreducible minimum of our faith. The once and future Christ is our message because the core of the gospel is the resurrection.

Where, then, do we begin in this hunt for the risen Christ? I suggest we have to start by assuring ourselves that we won't draw any *a priori* conclusions about the resurrection, like 'dead men don't rise, so the resurrection of Jesus didn't happen'. We have to look at the evidence and then make a measured decision, while recognizing that nothing can finally prove the resurrection. Even if we were to discover new evidence somehow confirming the empty tomb or the appearances of the risen Lord, those incidents in themselves would still be open to more than one interpretation. As the philosopher Wittgenstein said, 'It is love that believes the resurrection.' This doesn't mean that history doesn't matter; there still has to be an event to interpret. It's just that the event isn't quite like, 'In 2016 the UK decided to leave the European Union,' or, 'The 2020 Olympics are in Tokyo.' The experience of the risen Jesus led Thomas to say not, 'That's really quite interesting,' but rather, 'My Lord and my God.' This is an event of a different quality altogether.

It's obvious something of full and final significance happened here; the difficulty is in knowing precisely what that was. Indeed, 'precisely' is what we will never know. This is mystery in the best sense of something for us to deepen and enrich, rather than something for us to flatten out and explain. Sometimes it seems to me that the resurrection is best looked at as you look at a view when the light is too bright and you have to screw up your eyes to see. A full frontal view is too harsh; some restraint helps. A more nuanced and subtle approach to resurrection gives a richer understanding.

But let's look at what we're told by the people closest to the event.

The Gospels are unique documents in their style and intent, and when they get to the resurrection they're in totally uncharted territory. No longer do they reference the Old Testament; they're striking out on unknown paths. And, not surprisingly, they differ in their accounts. For example:

- How many women were involved – two (Matthew), three (Mark), several (Luke) or one (John)?
- Had the stone already been rolled away before the women got there (Mark, Luke, John) or were the women there when it happened (Matthew)?
- How many angels were there – one (Matthew and Mark) or two (Luke and John)?
- Was there some communication from the angel(s) on the first visit to the tomb (Matthew, Mark and Luke), or not (John)?
- Did the women tell the other disciples (Matthew, Luke, John) or not (Mark)?
- Who else was at the tomb apart from the women – 'the beloved disciple' and Peter (John), the guards (Matthew), nobody (Mark and Luke)?

So it's all a bit confusing. Some people try to make a consecutive narrative out of these complexities and smooth out the differences, but that's to miss the point. Those very inconsistencies are one of the best arguments that what we're dealing with here are first-hand accounts, passed on with care and reverence. It's the sort of thing that happens when different people with contrasting allegiances go to the same football match; they report it as they see it, but they see it differently.

If we're to go on a manhunt for Jesus after the resurrection, these are some of the things we should look at.

## The empty tomb

The Gospels are unanimous about this. The tomb was empty. The question is, why? Had the body been stolen? If so, by whom? If it were the disciples wanting to keep the body of their special friend safe, they were highly unlikely to keep up the deception to the point of the martyrdom they nearly all suffered. If it were the Jewish or Roman authorities wanting to prevent a cult of veneration growing up around Jesus, they would surely have produced the body when things started to get out of hand. Body snatchers, perhaps? The disciples clearly didn't believe that, and the authorities never pointed the finger at such a reason when rumours of a resurrection started circulating. This kind of manhunt would get nowhere.

Interestingly, there was no evidence of veneration at this special site for at least three centuries, in spite of the fact that reverence at holy places was common at the time (though understandably subdued because of the threat of persecution). The deeper truth was that the risen Jesus was to be found all over the place so there was no need to go to a tomb. It's striking that if you go to any of the great shrines – Rome for St Peter, Durham for St Cuthbert, Assisi for St Francis – you'll find the bones of the saint at the heart of the church. But when you go to Jerusalem you find an empty tomb.

Another fact to put into the balance is that the Gospel accounts credit women with being the first witnesses to this empty tomb, and these are precisely the people who would be least likely to be believed in that culture at that time. It's just an example of the authentic quality of the Gospel accounts, which come across as urgent, dramatic, breathless, believable.

## The appearances of Jesus

Here again we're in mysterious territory. Jesus is reported as having been seen over an extended period of time, by a variety of people, in a number of places – in the garden, in the upper room, on a late-afternoon walk to Emmaus, by the seashore in Galilee, on a mountain-top, and, as Paul reports, by more than five hundred people at one time (1 Corinthians 15.6). What do we make of all this? Was it imagination, wish fulfilment, hallucination?

Some people have seen these experiences not so much as real appearances but as shared memory, in effect a spiritual, non-material resurrection. In this account of things, the disciples shared and remembered what Jesus meant to them, and found themselves so emboldened by this communal memory that they went off confidently to preach about the kingdom and the special life of Jesus. Jesus' spirit was thereby 'resurrected' among them. But the facts recorded in the Gospels don't bear this out. The disciples were shattered and deeply fearful for their own future safety; they were hardly sitting around and becoming confident, world-changing apostles. Something tangible and incontrovertible had happened.

What about hallucination? That seems unlikely, given the number and variety of the appearances. Moreover, Jewish believers weren't simple people and they knew the difference between, on the one hand, dreams such as those of Joseph and Daniel in their Scriptures, and on the other the experience they had shared of Jesus eating fish with them (Luke 24.42) and inviting Thomas to touch his wounds (John 20.27). This had been their friend all right, not an hallucination.

The earliest testimony to the appearances of Jesus comes in Paul's correspondence with the church in Corinth. He would have written his first letter around AD 55, only 25 or so years after the events themselves, so when he says that most of the five hundred witnesses are still alive he's really saying, 'Check it out with them if you don't believe me.'

However, these appearances are nothing if not mysterious. Why do the disciples usually fail to recognize the risen Lord? Mary Magdalene didn't recognize Jesus in the garden, the followers of Jesus didn't recognize him as they walked home to Emmaus, the disciples on the lake didn't recognize him as he called out to them from the shore and made them breakfast. It's weird; this is Jesus, who they've spent so much time with, day and night, eating and joking, walking the hills and talking by the fire, captivated by his stories, and awed by his unselfconscious authority. And if not recognizing one of your best friends isn't enough, how could Jesus sometimes materialize and later vanish when the disciples were in lock-down for fear of being discovered?

So what did Jesus look like after the resurrection? We have no idea. But perhaps it helps if we realize that Jesus hadn't simply been revived or resuscitated like Lazarus; he had been raised to what needs to be called a 'glorified body', that is, one that is both physical (he still had a body) and also wonderfully transformed. This body had been created afresh by God, the first sign of a new creation, a body that would never die. If this seems paradoxical or even contradictory, we might get the merest glimpse of what it could mean if we think of talking with a new mother soon after the birth of her baby. If asked, she might say the experience was wonderful – but also frighten-ing. 'So which was it?' we might say. 'Wonderful or frightening?' 'Both,' she would answer. Of course. The descriptions might seem contradictory but they're both true. Was the resurrec-tion body of Jesus physical or spiritual? Both. This was the first experience of a new world. Of course the description of Jesus might be confusing. At least in the case of giving birth there's precedent, but to what can the experience of the risen Christ be compared? It was unique. A conventional manhunt would have been a waste of time.

So now we have two key pieces of evidence concerning the reality of the resurrection. Each needs the other. An empty tomb with no appearances would have left people thinking of a stolen body. Appearances without an empty tomb would have left people thinking of the wish fulfilment of the bereaved. Taken together, they represent mounting evidence. But there's more.

## The transformed disciples

It's hard to identify the village of Emmaus. There are three or four contenders, but when you've been to Abu Ghosh you feel that if this isn't it, it should be. The present Benedictine sanc-tuary was built by the Crusaders over a crypt given its shape by the walls of a Roman reservoir. The quiet church has a simple strength and serenity paralleled only by St Anne's in Jerusalem. It's a beautiful place to have a Eucharist at the end of a pilgrim-age. The acoustic makes your little group sound like a crowd of hundreds. The walls have soaked up prayer and given back peace. 'Here might I stay and sing . . .'

The story of the two followers of Jesus walking back to Emmaus that Sunday afternoon is deservedly a favourite. One was Cleopas; the other was either another male disciple or possibly his wife Mary. The bottom had fallen out of their world; they were utterly depressed. The hopes they had had that 'he was the one to redeem Israel' (Luke 24.21) were now laughable – except they weren't laughing, they were simply dragging their weary minds and bodies back home. They were walking away from Jerusalem and maybe even walking away from their faith in Jesus. Then Jesus joined them on the road. He explained the Scriptures to them, and later he broke bread in their home, and suddenly their known world lurched totally off course. They were shocked and thrilled beyond measure. It was him!

What we see in those disciples as they run, skip and jump back to Jerusalem is what happened to all the disciples as the impossible burst upon them. They simply hadn't been expecting resurrection. They knew of the hope of resurrection for the whole people of Israel at the end of history, on the last day, but the idea of someone being raised in the middle of history was just not in anyone's mind. And yet here was this undeniable experience crashing into their lives from a cloudless sky. It was a classic 'before and after'. 'Before' they were broken and demoralized, awaiting a similar dire fate to Jesus. 'After', as we see in Acts, they're joyfully and fearlessly telling everyone what they've seen and known. These are the self-same people. Acts is only Luke a few weeks on. Jerusalem is the same frightening place. But now they're ready to be arrested, harassed, beaten up, martyred – and nothing will stop them.

Something huge happened to these men and women. Something like resurrection.

## The existence of the Church

One of the most noticeable things about pilgrimage in the Holy Land these days is the massive increase in the number of pilgrims coming from the Far East. As I wander through the holy sites I see wave after wave of groups from Korea, Hong Kong and Singapore, as well as groups from Africa, Eastern Europe and elsewhere. Truly the Church is alive and growing. There are 2.3 billion people around the world who name Christ as the one they follow, and that number is growing at the rate of 70,000 every day of the year.

Again, something remarkable must have caused and sustained all this. Without the resurrection we would simply have had another failed messiah, a jumped-up preacher who overreached himself and was brushed off the Pax Romana like any other irritant. It's estimated that 2,000 people had been crucified in Palestine in the single year 4 BC, when Jesus had just been born. Jesus would simply have been another wretch like those, paying the price for his insolence.

But the Jesus movement was utterly different. Within 300 years the whole Roman edifice had fallen under the spell of this itinerant prophet from Galilee. What can account for such an impact? Surely not something based on a lie or a mistake. The resurrection and the continuing life of the risen Christ in his Church is the only causative factor big enough to account for this astonishing story, one that still gets richer by the day.

## Lived experience

Mr Wrigley was a quiet, undemonstrative Lancastrian who gave out the hymn books and took the collection at the church where my father was vicar. He didn't smile much and he didn't stay for coffee. I'm not sure I ever identified Mrs Wrigley. But once a year Mr Wrigley came into his own. On Easter Day he would march down the length of this large church and present himself at the vicar's vestry. He would stand in the doorway and say to my father, 'Christ is risen, Vicar.' And my father would reply, 'He is risen indeed, Mr Wrigley.' Mr Wrigley would nod, obviously satisfied with the answer, and then he would set off for the back of the church again for the rest of the year.

I used to love that exchange because somehow it encapsulated Mr Wrigley's faith. Here was this stolid Christian man, one who would probably never go to a house group or pray aloud or lead the intercessions, giving witness to the core belief that sustained him as he did his job, loved his wife, paid his taxes and gave out hymn books in church. Christ was risen and so everything else would fit into place. It was his lived experience – articulated just once a year.

I could no more deny my experience of the living Christ than deny my love of my children. And this is what sustains millions of Christians living in hugely different circumstances all over the globe. In some way, some more vivid than others, some more opaque and searching, some more activist, some more contemplative, some more analytical, some more emotional – in some way those millions of Christians have known the presence of the risen Christ.

It's also astonishing to see how within a few years of his death the people who had known Jesus best had recalibrated their understanding and experience of Jesus. They had been with him in the ordinary experiences of living together on the road, including, presumably, when he was tired out, when he twisted his ankle, when he dropped the dinner plates, when he got frustrated with the stall-holder trying to cheat him, as well as when his compassion seemed boundless, his preaching soared, and his healings left people astounded. But now, this short time later, these same friends of his were giving him all sorts of exalted titles. Typically, like Paul, they called him Lord, which Greek-speaking Jews would only use when referring to God. This was astonishing for fiercely monotheistic Jews. It seems that from now on the disciples would never again think or speak of Jesus without thinking and speaking of God. Philippians 2.5–11 demonstrates how truly remarkable this reframing was. Only a risen Christ could justify such an extravagant use of words.

Lived experience, then, both in the early Church and in our own lives now, invites us to recognize the presence of the risen Christ. Mr Wrigley had put his finger on it.

The manhunt for Jesus has continued since the day of his baptism. At first he was pursued by the crowds, then by the Jewish authorities, and then by the Romans, who finally nailed him down. Or not. Because when the manhunt began for the mysterious risen Christ, he was never caught, except by those he caught himself, in a garden, in an upper room, on a country road, on a Galilean shore. And the manhunt continues to this day, as people seek the elusive Stranger who, in the famous words of Albert Schweitzer:

comes to us as One unknown, without a name, as of old, by the lakeside, he came to those men who knew him not. He speaks to us in the same words: 'Follow me' and sets us to the tasks which he has to fulfil for our time. He commands. And to those who obey him, whether they be wise or simple, he will reveal himself in the toils, the conflicts, the sufferings which they shall pass through in his fellowship, and, as an ineffable mystery, they shall learn *in their own experience,* who he is.[2]

Seeing isn't always believing. But love is.

# 9

## The manhunt: what does it mean?

The shoreline at the church of St Peter's Primacy on the Sea of Galilee is one that calls me back time and again. It's the place where tradition says that Jesus had breakfast with the seven disciples who had gone back to Galilee to pick up the threads of their old life because they couldn't work out what to do with the intermittent appearances of Jesus in Jerusalem. The city held nothing for them long term, so at Peter's suggestion they went home. On that misty morning Jesus called out from the beach to the frustrated fishermen who had caught nothing all night. They took his advice and were overwhelmed with the catch, but still unsure whether this was really Jesus. Full of curiosity and wonder, they came ashore and Jesus gave them breakfast. I imagine him humming a psalm as he cooked the fish and handed it around, with the disciples not knowing what to say and eating in embarrassed silence, remembering their own defections in Gethsemane. But fellowship was being restored, especially when Jesus took Peter to one side and assured him that there were no hard feelings about his denials and he was still trusted to lead the way forward.

When you go to that beach now the sea may well be quite a long way out from the little chapel, with the 'breakfast rock' spilling over from the beach right into the sanctuary. Go there in the afternoon when the pilgrim groups have gone through and you have it almost to yourself. You can sit there looking out at the sea and the contours of the hills opposite, seeing just what Jesus saw so long ago, listening to the gentle lapping of the sea on the stones, and sometimes, if you're lucky, seeing two men wading into the water and casting their nets in the timeless manner that concertinas the time of Jesus and our own time. You can sit on a rock on the water's edge, the sun pouring down, your Bible open at John 21. The risen Christ can't be far away.

The manhunt that follows the resurrection is the hunt for meaning. What does this stunning event mean, both then and now? Of course, it's an event that couldn't have happened. But that's the point. It's so outrageous it could change everything, and does. With our finite minds we're unlikely to be able to make adequate sense of an infinite experience, one with such far-reaching implications. We're like an ant crawling around the foot of an elephant trying to work out exactly what's going on with the enormous reality up above. But that doesn't permit us to give up the struggle to understand; we can't leave our rational minds in the waiting room. We have to let evidence and analysis take us as far as they can – and then try to go a little further to the place where the rational gives way to the supra-rational, the arena of God's freedom and grace. We won't ever fully understand the Author of existence but we can speculate and imagine. Hamlet will never understand the mind of Shakespeare because he's the creation of the author and therefore in a different order of existence, but that doesn't stop him thinking and dreaming within his own sphere of understanding.

So what does the resurrection mean?

## The cross is a victory, not a defeat

That Good Friday night everything looked pretty grim. Jesus was no more, the light had been extinguished. The disciples were hiding out wherever they could, many of them in that upper room, so poignant with memory. The women were shell-shocked after what they'd seen that day, but they could at least prepare the spices to anoint the precious body. It was all disastrous; the Galilean dream was shattered.

But on Sunday morning the future crashed into the present and everything was suddenly up for reimagination. What had seemed like gross defeat became glorious victory. Former Archbishop Michael Ramsey said, 'The crucifixion is not a defeat needing the resurrection to reverse it, but a victory which the resurrection quickly follows and seals.' The cross was Easter in disguise, though they couldn't know it at the time. In mythological terms which hide a deep truth, Jesus had taken on the powers of darkness and absorbed them in the light of God's profound presence. Evil had done its worst, spent its anger, and lost. The result is as poet and theologian Malcolm Guite puts it: 'In a daring and beautiful reversal, God takes the worst we can do to him and turns it into the very best he can do for us.'[1]

So the cross turns out to be a victory. As Paul puts it, 'He disarmed the rulers and authorities and made a public example of them, triumphing over them' (Colossians 2.15). It was an image beloved of the early Church Fathers too. But in between the cross and the resurrection is a profound, unbridgeable gap. It's a real, dark space that as far as the disciples were concerned might have gone on for ever. There was no automatic happy ending but a huge, logical abyss that could only be broken by an utterly new, unexpected act of God. We don't really grasp the reality of that gap today, so used are we to seeing the cross and resurrection belonging together, joined at the hip. But at the time these were two stories, not one story in two acts. Only later did we see how God's love was consistent throughout. The resurrection then revealed what had in fact been the glorious victory of the cross.

## In particular, death is defeated

Death is so serious that we sometimes try to handle it with humour. Woody Allen's famous quip is often quoted: 'I'm not afraid of death; I just don't want to be there when it happens.' We smile at the funeral director who signed his letter, 'Yours eventually'. But death is the dark wind blowing from the future of each one of us and it seems to blow randomly and recklessly, leaving us all frightened. It's like background music playing softly throughout our lives, sometimes swelling in volume and intensity until we manage to control it again, but always there.

However, death met its match on the cross. It seemed to score its ultimate victory, the death of the Son of God, but it turned out to be its definitive defeat. The best commentary on this defeat is found in 1 Corinthians 15 where Paul spells out the implications for those who live in Christ. 'Death has been swallowed up in victory. Where, O death, is your victory?

Where, O death, is your sting?' (15. 54–55). To continue the mythological imagery of this victory, C. S. Lewis wrote: 'Jesus has forced open a door that has been locked since the death of the first man. He has met, fought and beaten the King of Death. Everything is different because he has done so.'[2]

The point of this victory is that if the dreaded wall of death has been breached at one place it's been breached fatally and for ever. Never again can it be claimed that death has the last word. For those who are 'in Christ', death is a busted flush. That doesn't make the prospect and process of dying any more attractive but it relativizes it, and ensures that Christians have a different outlook on death. As an atheist, the philosopher Bertrand Russell was bound to see the future beyond death as being without hope. 'There is darkness without and when I die there will be darkness within. There is no splendour, no vastness anywhere, only triviality for a moment and then nothing.'[3] Christians hold a completely different vision because, as they see it, death has been defeated on the cross and left powerless in the resurrection. Although death is still an enemy, it's now a defeated enemy.

## Jesus is vindicated as Messiah

There were plenty of false messiahs in Jesus' day. It was a sign of the desperation of the Jewish people that they seized on any likely leader who might drive out the pagan invaders and restore the fortunes of Zion. It's possible to name at least 12 such messiahs in Jesus' time, and to record their inevitable deaths as they came up against the hard steel of Rome and the unforgiving wood of crucifixion. These were cruel times. And obviously a dead messiah rapidly lost his followers. No disciples continued to believe in their messiah after he was strung up and eliminated.

Who Jesus was had been disputed throughout his life. He had been called a prophet, a teacher, a rabbi, but was he the Messiah, the one who would show himself a great military leader just when it was needed? Jesus quickly dismissed any identification between himself and that kind of messiah, but he was more ambivalent about the underlying role. Only once is he recorded as accepting the title (Mark 14.62), though he came close in other Gospels ('Tell us if you are the Messiah, the Son of God' . . . 'You have said so' – Matthew 26.63). But he did many of the things that would be associated with the Messiah, such as forgiving sins, rewriting parts of the Jewish law, and saying that he would be involved in judging Israel on the Last Day. But essentially Jesus wanted people to make their own decision about who he was, to see it for themselves, and see also that he wasn't offering a conventional model of messiahship. Most obviously, of course, the expected Messiah would never suffer and die on a cross. What use would such a messiah be?

But the resurrection changed all that. Jesus' followers were galvanized into action and exploded into the world with their message of a risen Lord. Any doubt was removed. This wonderful leader of theirs had been vindicated by God. Jesus was undoubtedly the Messiah, and the Messiah wasn't the great military leader they had expected but a Man who said you win by losing, lead by serving, and live by dying. Moreover, he had done all of that himself.

Jesus has no competitors in the role of Messiah. In the French Revolution, the diplomat Talleyrand was approached by a young friend who was discouraged at not being able to establish a new religion after what he saw as the clear failure of Catholic Christianity. The young man asked Talleyrand's advice. The famous statesman said that it would be difficult, so difficult he hardly knew what to advise. 'Still,' he said, 'there is one thing you might at least try. I should recommend you be crucified and rise again on the third day.'

## We catch a glimpse of journey's end

When you're in the Holy Land you're two hours ahead of UK time and seven hours ahead of the east coast of the USA. I find I have to be careful phoning home when I'm there (though not as careful as when I'm in New Zealand). A thoughtless early-morning call home when on pilgrimage doesn't go down too well, I've found. The problem is that I'm in what you might call 'new time', ahead of what we might call 'old time', which is running a few hours behind. The resurrection is an introduction to new time.

Our whole world is still in old time, where the old weary ways still hold sway, and hatred and violence, tribalism and prejudice, evil and death remain all too evident. But in the risen Christ we have someone who has come to us from new time, having gone through the barrier of death into God's new world, God's new creation. He's come to tell us – still in old time – that the new day has dawned and even though we may feel sleepy and it still seems dark outside, the new world has in fact begun and it would be great if we woke up properly, and got to work on 'new world projects'. There are a number of parables in the Gospels about very early mornings and people getting ready for the bridegroom. In the resurrection appearances of Jesus the new creation temporarily grazed against the old one. Jesus brought the good news of a new world and energized his followers to get out there and start making the kingdom of God real, the new world in the old world.

God's new world is in fact a new heaven and a new earth, not a disembodied heaven ready for occupation after death. It's this world that will be renewed as heaven overlaps earth and the two will be as one. Tom Wright puts it this way:

> The present world is full of corruption and decay, of violence and sorrow and sin and death. But the whole point is that what God has decided to do about all this – precisely because he's the Creator who loves the world he made – is to do away with all that corruption and sorrow and death, and so leave the way clear for the world to be renewed from top to bottom, so that everything that's pure and lovely and beautiful and noble and wise will shine all the more brightly. That is the future world which we are promised, and which the ancient Jewish people were already promised in their scriptures.[4]

What happened with Jesus is that God brought the plan forward so that instead of this renewal of creation being inaugurated at the end of history it happened in the middle, and the resurrection is the sign that God's new creation has now begun. Not only has a phone call come in from new time to old time but Someone from new time has turned up on the doorstep.

Former Archbishop Rowan Williams used similar imagery of a new creation when he wrote: 'When we celebrate Easter we are really standing in the middle of a second Big Bang, a tumultuous surge of divine energy as fiery and intense as the very beginning of the universe.'[5] In the resurrection we see the ground plan of the new world, one that isn't a pale, fluffy version of the old one, but a full-blooded re-creation of it, one that we call the kingdom of God. In the cross and resurrection Jesus took creation with him through the decay of death and out the other side, beyond the reach of death. Paul has a vivid picture of what's been happening until now when he says that creation has been groaning in labour pains for its new birth (Romans 8.22). Now, at last, we've seen the point of all this 'groaning'; a new world is on its way.

## Christ is alive, through the Spirit

It may be difficult to understand but you have to admit that it's logical. If Christ rose again then he's alive. He didn't die again like Lazarus. He returned to the Father (we'll look at what that means in Chapters 11–13). Someone I know well thought hard about this issue when she was coming to faith. She reasoned that if Christ has been raised from the dead then he must still be alive, and if he was alive he could in some sense be known, and if he could be known he could be her friend. But what does that really mean? Paul was sure that he wanted 'to know Christ and the power of his resurrection' (Philippians 3.10), but how can you know someone who lived 2,000 years ago?

Perhaps it helps to think of a spectrum of interpretations of what it means. At one end is the basic understanding of knowing Christ as a friend who can be part of our lives and a partner in our conversations (prayer). I realize that the idea of Jesus as a friend runs the risk of sentimentality, and indeed of trivialization. It can seem too direct, too literal, and lacking respect. Is there a danger of thinking of Jesus as a charming friend, as we might have done when we were children? To make Jesus a friend may be to denigrate the significance and authority of the risen Christ. But we have to bear in mind that for huge numbers of people 'friend' seems like the best description of their relationship with the Divine. Even Gregory of Nyssa, one of the early Church Fathers, is supposed to have said, as his last words, 'The most important thing is to become God's friend.' Moses is said to have spoken with God, 'as one speaks to a friend' (Exodus 33.11). This is the way many people frame and express their encounters with the God we see in Jesus. When I first found a faith for myself, having a personal relationship with Christ was the defining difference in my 'before and after' experience.

Further along the spectrum of interpretations of 'knowing Christ' is knowing him as the compelling, fascinating, enigmatic figure at the centre of our thinking about faith and what it means for daily living. Here is the Person around whom to shape our values and behaviour. This is the Christ of that maligned but useful question, 'What would Jesus do?' – a figure with whom to align ourselves, or wrestle, or imagine a better world, one in whose company we can interrogate society's idols and fantasies. The person of Christ is endlessly absorbing.

Further along the spectrum again, we might think of 'knowing Christ' in a more allusive, tangential way as the central, loving, teasing divine presence in our Christian lives. Here Christ is more opaque and perhaps more fused with God the Father. We live in an atmosphere of 'Christfulness' and are aware of the spirit of Christ rather more than the person of Christ. It's a more contemplative vision of knowing Christ.

For myself I think I identify with all three positions on that spectrum – the personal relationship with Christ, the total fascination with Jesus, and the allusive presence of Christ. Perhaps the important thing is not to overanalyse what 'knowing Christ' means but to enjoy it. His concern, after all, is chiefly with what will break the ice around our hearts, not the mechanics of it.

And what really matters is for us to realize that the New Testament has all sorts of images for this 'relationship' with X. Most often used is our being 'in Christ'. '*En Christo*' occurs throughout Paul's letters. But there's also 'coming to Christ' (John 6.37), 'receiving Christ' (Revelation 3.20), Christ living in the believer (Galatians 2.20), following Christ (the initial call of the disciples and Jesus with Peter and John when Peter is being recommissioned after the resurrection). There's no one image of this relationship. The vital thing, according to the New Testament, is X and the believer coming together.

More and more I think simply of being a follower of Jesus. As the Jews had it, I want to be 'covered in the dust of my rabbi'.

Whatever words we use, the deep security that we are offered is that we are never alone. This isn't the same as saying that we are kept from harm. In a world of cause and effect, of action and interaction, of chance and necessity, bad things may well happen to us. It's the way the world is, and has to be, if we're to be genuinely free. *But we will never be alone in whatever happens* – that's the promise. And it's the promise of presence that makes all the difference. If there's a raging storm in the night and you go to be with your scared young child; if someone is approaching death and the time for words is past; if someone has to go to court and is scared of going alone – in these situations it's *presence* that matters more than anything.

In a speech he gave in the House of Commons in 2012 Colonel Bob Stewart recounted an experience of going to the aid of a young woman just after an IRA bomb had gone off. She was lying on the ground with her legs gone and her arm a wreck. He knelt down beside her. She said, 'What happened?' He said, 'There's been an explosion, darling.' 'Am I hurt?' she asked. He said, 'Quite a bit.' She said, 'Am I badly hurt?' He said, 'Yes, you are.' 'Am I going to die?' she asked. 'Yes,' he said gently. She replied simply, 'Will you hold me?'

We have the promise of God's presence, God's 'holding', whether we focus our thinking on the Father, on Jesus, or on the Spirit of both. The living Christ is always right there. If it's not too simple, in the words of an old song, 'You've got a friend.'

It's also worth reflecting on the experience and practice of the Church, which wouldn't begin to make sense if Christ were not alive. If Christ were not our contemporary we would *read the Bible* simply as a historical document rather than as a living Word for us today. We would have *an initiation ceremony* very different from one that sees believers as being incorporated into the life, death and new life of Jesus. We would have *a commemoration meal* like many illustrious institutions, but wouldn't think of it as receiving the very life of Christ. The bottom-line assumption behind every action characteristic of the Church is that Christ is alive and can be experienced in our lives today.

But we've already begun to anticipate the third section of our exploration of the manhunt – what does all this mean for us now as we try to follow the living Jesus?

# 10

## *The manhunt:*
## *what does it mean for us now?*

Gerard Manley Hopkins was a nineteenth-century Jesuit priest whose poetry continues to dazzle us. In one of his poems he uses the evocative phrase, 'let him easter in us'.[1] Easter as a verb – that's intriguing. But it reflects the experience of the resurrection for millions of people. It's not a bare fact to file away under 'R'. It's a lived experience that changes and energizes lives, inspires sacrificial living, and fills the Church with hope.

When I lead retreats by the Sea of Galilee we end with a Eucharist by the water's edge on the morning of our departure. The view across the lake is the perfect backdrop; we're seeing what Jesus saw. We break bread on the lakeshore as Jesus did with his awestruck disciples after the resurrection. We sing and pray and concentrate fiercely as we try to imprint this place on our memories before leaving it behind. Staying for a week by the northwestern corner of the Sea of Galilee where Jesus spent so much of his time, reading and reflecting on the stories in the places where they happened, praying and journalling, eating and sleeping, and all of this done spaciously, without having to dash off to the next holy site – all that leaves a holy mark on every soul. But then we pack up and board a coach to take us to Tel Aviv airport and gradually the magical morning fades. We're caught up in traffic and crowds and queues and the probing questions of airport security. We're immersed in twenty-first-century life, full of anxiety, consumerism and digital communication, and we wonder if it can only have been this morning that we were sharing Communion by the Sea of Galilee.

However, the difference between this visit and our other holidays, wherever they may be, is that this retreat isn't just a delicious memory but a living encounter with the God who disclosed himself in Jesus and who, in a courteous but penetrating way, asks us what we're going to do about the experience we've just had. The focus of our Communion service has been the resurrection, and the resurrection has implications. They're demanding implications, certainly, but every one of them is good.

## Easter is our touchstone

At the end of *The Lord of the Rings*, Frodo and Sam are recovering from their wounds and in a deep sleep. Gandalf wakes Sam, who says:

> 'Gandalf! I thought you were dead! But then I thought I was dead myself. Is everything sad going to come untrue? What's happening to the world?'
>
> 'A great Shadow has departed,' said Gandalf, and then he laughed, and the sound was like music, or like water in a parched land; and as he listened the thought came to Sam that he had not heard laughter, the pure sound of merriment, for days upon days without count. It fell upon his ears like the echo of all the joys he had ever known. But he himself burst into tears. Then, as a sweet rain will pass down a wind of spring and the sun will shine out the clearer, his tears ceased, and his laughter welled up, and laughing he sprang from his bed.
>
> 'How do I feel?' he cried. 'Well, I don't know how to say it. I feel, I feel' – he waved his arms in the air – 'I feel like spring after winter, and sun on the leaves; and like trumpets and harps and all the songs I have ever heard!'[2]

That sounds like resurrection to me. It's no wonder J. R. R. Tolkien, who wrote those words, also wrote that the resurrection is 'a joy beyond the walls of the world, poignant as grief'.[3] Resurrection is the game-changer for the Christian. In its light everything looks different, and in the risen Christ we are always somehow at the beginning of life with so much before us. But it's 'beyond the walls of the world'; it's not something you can compute or predict. Resurrection can jump out and surprise us in a conversation with a friend, a lover's touch, a view down a Lakeland valley, a piece of music that tears at the heart – we never know when we might be ambushed by grace. When people fall in love or receive wonderful news they don't sit slumped in front of the television or peel potatoes or clean the bathroom; they sing and dance and feel they've been given five aces. The joy of the resurrection is like that.

But did you notice that Sam also burst into tears? Was it relief, or the release of pent-up emotion, or simply another way of expressing joy? Maybe it was the result of a long period of living in the dark and at long last seeing a shaft of light streaking into his life. It's worth remembering that the resurrection happened in darkness, like so many other events of ultimate significance in God's story – creation, the birth of Jesus, the crucifixion, now the resurrection before dawn. We usually go over the top on Easter Day with flowers, streamers, great music, everything ablaze with light. But the resurrection happened in a cave, in silence, in darkness, with the stale smell of earth and stone. Resurrection might be a hard, slow process for some, with tears and struggle, 'poignant as grief'.

I'm moved by the two paintings of the supper at Emmaus by Caravaggio. His painting of 1601, when Roman society smiled upon him, is full of light and colour, the fresh fruit falling off the table into our hands, amazement shining through every brushstroke. His painting of 1606 is quite different. He's on the run from papal authority, having got into a fatal brawl, and he's desperately trying to curb his propensity for violence and return to favour. This painting shows that the resurrection came at great cost; the colours are restrained, the figures are dark and gaunt, the fare on the table is meagre. This resurrection meal is a struggle.

Easter might be our touchstone as Christians but it won't do to over-claim for the resurrection. The Christian life isn't all champagne and strawberries, but even when it's lived in shadows and struggle, the resurrection is our centre point. We are an Easter people, basing our faith solidly on the resurrection and knowing the encouragement of the living Christ who 'easters' in us. A core biblical verse for me has always been, 'I came that they may have life, and have it abundantly' (John 10.10), and the resurrection is the key to that abundance as the life of God floods the world. Another core text I've long enjoyed reflects that focus on life, but this time it comes from the prophetic episcopal pen of John V. Taylor:

> It has long been my conviction that God is not hugely concerned as to whether we are religious or not. What matters to God, and matters supremely, is whether we are alive or not. If your religion brings you more fully to life, God will be in it; but if your religion inhibits your capacity for life, you may be sure God is against it, just as Jesus was.[4]

I wish I'd thought of those words first. For Christians, the life and light that pours from an empty tomb is our springboard into faith.

## We have new personal priorities

If the resurrection takes root in our lives we can't go on living as we did before. The moral implications of the living Christ being let loose in the world are deeply significant, and Paul points them out in no uncertain terms in many places, including in his letter to the Colossians. Halfway through the letter he says, 'So if you have been raised with Christ, seek the things that are above, where Christ is, seated at the right hand of God' (Colossians 3.1). We are to set our priorities on God's things, not our own, 'things that are above, not things that are on earth' (3.2). This will involve putting to death a whole list of destructive actions and attitudes (3.5–9: not an encouraging list when it was read on Easter morning), and instead, to 'clothe' ourselves with compassion, kindness, humility, meekness and patience. We are to bear with each other's foibles and failings for the very good reason that we ourselves have been forgiven. Then Paul comes to a climax with the instruction to 'clothe yourselves with love, which binds everything together' (3.12–14).

I'm fond of that image of 'clothing' ourselves with love. It's very vivid and memorable, particularly when a preacher does actually clothe himself with a surplice, as I once saw someone do in a pulpit to illustrate the effectiveness of deliberately putting on the ways of Christ. I can see him still. It would have been even better if he could have illustrated Romans 12.2 because that's where Paul goes further. 'Do not be conformed to this world but be transformed by the renewing of your minds.' That's an even deeper change than putting on love, compassion, kindness; it's a profound inner change of character.

How this works out is another subject for another book, but here the point to note is that in the light of the resurrection we have a different starting point for the way we live. We start from the 'things that are above', God's ways, which involve a radical rescheduling of our priorities away from self-absorption and personal gain, and towards the well-being of others. Jesus is our guide on this, with his teaching on the kingdom and the Sermon on the Mount. He was no pushover plaster saint but the love of God made flesh, utterly focused on his Father, ready to go wherever love called.

If we love like that, hopefully we'll leave behind a trail of empty tombs.

## We have an agenda for change

You can't visit Israel/Palestine without longing for change. When I take groups there I make sure we're exposed to the social and political realities that beset the lives of citizens of both communities. There are representatives of the Parents Circle to meet, where parents from both sides of the divide who've lost children in the country's violence have committed themselves to work together for reconciliation, starting with their own relationship. There are members of Breaking the Silence, former Jewish soldiers who want to tell their story of how they were made to treat Palestinians when they were in the military. But there are also Settlers to meet who can't understand why rockets are regularly fired out of Gaza at Israeli cities. Christians are pincered in the midst of these deeply entrenched positions, but they have an indomitable commitment to peace and justice, and often have a bigger impact than their small numbers would suggest was possible.

Christians have an agenda for change because in a sense we belong to the future. We should be people from 'new time', the world as God is making it, so that ultimately the earth will fill out the meaning of Jesus' enigmatic phrase, 'the kingdom of God'. Jesus announced and inaugurated a new social order, and demonstrated it in the way he lived. It was, and still is, a clear alternative to the established way of violence, exclusion and inequality. We claim, therefore, to be people with a new vision of how we can live together, even though for now we inevitably live in something like Holy Saturday, between profound disappointment (the Good Fridays of life) and intoxicating hope (the Easter Days). And this hope isn't of the whistling-in-the-dark variety. It's based on a sober estimate of what the Roman Catholic writer Ronald Rolheiser calls 'the deep moral structure of the universe' revealed in the resurrection. He offers this analysis of what the resurrection discloses:

> The contours of the universe are love and goodness and truth, and this structure, anchored at its centre by Ultimate Love and Power, is non-negotiable: You live life its way or it simply won't come out right. More importantly, the reverse is also true: If you respect the structure [of the universe] and live life its way, what's good and true and loving will eventually triumph, always, despite everything. If this is true, and it is, then we don't have to escape pain and death to achieve victory – we've only to remain faithful, good, and true inside of them.[5]

If this seems unduly optimistic, let's come down to earth a bit more. The materiality of the resurrection body of Jesus – whatever was also its spiritual nature – means that the ordinary stuff of life matters. The resurrection body was no amorphous spirit, drifting around Jerusalem until called to higher things. The material world is part of God's pleasure. Indeed, Gregory of Nazianzus tells us that 'what is not assumed is not healed'; that is, what is not taken into God's life can't be transformed by God, so every part of creation is important. Christians therefore will work for the transformation of everything – politics, business, the financial system, the law, the internet, the arts, environmental policy, international relations, education, family life and so on. Our agenda is to remake, transform and heal all human life under God.

Inevitably there is opposition to such an agenda, some of it from within the Church and much of it from outside. People tell us to restrict ourselves to 'spiritual' matters, as if the flourishing of men and women, and their communities and nations, wasn't of concern to God. This resistance is nicely summed up in a passage from Oscar Wilde's play *Salome* where Herod is quite happy with Jesus healing people but is horrified at him raising the dead. 'I do not wish him to do that,' says Herod. 'I forbid him to do that. I allow no man to raise the dead. This man must be found and told that I forbid him to raise the dead. Where is this man?' A courtier replies, 'He is in every place, my Lord, but it is hard to find him.'

How much more is that the case after the resurrection. The risen Christ is everywhere; it's hard to pin him down but (metaphorically speaking) he keeps on raising the dead.

## We can approach death confidently

My father-in-law died recently. He had achieved 95 years of 'ordinary' living. Nothing spectacular, except that he had lived and loved well, sustaining his family, working conscientiously, supporting his church (and in football, York City), and facing every challenge with wonderful equanimity and patience. He had been in the terrible Russian convoys in the war and moored off the beaches on D-Day, but you'd never have known of such courage if he hadn't written about those events at our request. And then he died. We were with him, praying him on his way, when he seemed to decide to stop breathing, and life left his body and everything was peaceful. That ordinary, extraordinary life had come to an end. Death exudes finality.

This is one of the most significant tests of a resurrection faith, whether it be the death of a loved one, a tragic world event, or our own sinking below the horizon of life. I hope I shall be confident of God's love and my future in it when my turn comes, but I don't know. None of us knows. John Shea put it beautifully: 'What the resurrection teaches us is not how to live, but how to live again, and again, and again.'[6] But ultimately those 'agains' have to be in a new life beyond this one.

The actor and comedian Eddie Izzard wrote that he was intent on living every day at full stretch because this is our one shot at life. He said that if only somebody, just one person, had come back to let us know that there was a life beyond this one, then everything would be different, but of course it's never happened. As I read this I thought, 'Hasn't he ever heard of the resurrection?' There are millions of people who have at the heart of their faith this stubborn, glorious fact of the resurrection of Jesus Christ from the dead. And so everything has changed.

In 1 Corinthians 15 Paul makes the case for an inescapable link between the resurrection of Jesus and our own resurrection.

> Now if Christ is proclaimed as raised from the dead, how can some of you say there is no resurrection of the dead? If there is no resurrection of the dead, then Christ has not been raised . . . But in fact Christ has been raised from the dead, the first fruits of those who have died.
> (1 Corinthians 15.12–13, 20)

He goes on to speculate on the nature of the resurrection body, using the metaphor of a seed that dies in the ground in one form, and emerges in due course in a quite different form (15.35–44). So he reaches the conclusion that we will have what he calls a 'spiritual body'.

Jesus never goes that far. He gives us many instances of a heavenly banquet but doesn't speculate on the details of life after death. How could he have known, given the particularity of the incarnation, being born at one place and time? What he had, however, was complete confidence in the love of his Father, so he could leave it in God's hands, even facing the nightmare of the cross. God would vindicate, somehow, what he had been doing. I don't think he could have known that his resurrection would take place as it did, or why would he have tried to avoid death in Gethsemane? If he knew he would be back so soon and so gloriously he would presumably have felt differently about the cross. Indeed, if he had been certain about the inevitability of his resurrection the cross would have been an elaborate deception. But what he assuredly did know was that his Father would never let him down and that somehow his death would lead to the future that he had come to announce and inaugurate.

We tend to use the word 'heaven' when we think about the future beyond death, but we use this expression carelessly. Tom Wright constantly tries to relativize the idea that we 'go to heaven' on our death. That's true as far as it goes, but it's even more important to realize, he says, that the New Testament writers were pointing to nothing less than new heavens and a new earth. They weren't simply saying that believers would go to heaven. And in any case, it isn't some surviving 'soul' that God takes to himself. That's a Greek rather than a Jewish idea. For the Jews, and therefore for the first Christians, death was death; there wasn't a little bit of us that would hang on. But God would raise the faithful from the depths of death, and give them a brand new life. Resurrection, not resuscitation. Jesus, not Lazarus.

We can approach death confidently. Cardinal Basil Hume discovered he had cancer and only had a few weeks to live. He phoned his good friend the Abbot of Ampleforth, who said straight back, 'Congratulations! I wish I could come with you.' That may be a little over the top for most of us. But the sentiment is good. We have nothing to fear in death, even if the process of dying remains a cause of anxiety.

## The Church needs to take on the character of Christ

It must have crossed the mind of every bishop and church leader that the Church isn't exactly fit for purpose in terms of engaging current and future generations of younger people with the gospel. Somehow we got left behind when individualism, the internet and the idolization of choice ganged up on institutions in general and Grand Narratives in particular. Too much church life has got stuck handling structures, procedures, authority and order, rather than the more faith-related issues of love, joy, peace, hope, meaning, justice, inclusion, vulnerability and so on.

The resurrection suggests that we need a risen Church for a risen Christ, and that means recovering something of the character of Christ himself – and replaying at least some of his core narrative of death and resurrection in the life of the Church. It means becoming again a movement of change-makers rather than a gated community of change-resisters. Jesus wasn't crucified for maintaining the status quo; he pushed all the boundaries, trying to establish the footprint of heaven on earth. Would he recognize the Church today as the vehicle of the kingdom that he hoped to leave behind?

A risen Church with the character of Christ would have the qualities of joyfulness, hospitality, flexibility, inclusion, care for the outsider, passion for justice and non-violence, and so much more. It would be made up of communities where people might stumble into God, where children buzzed and bloomed, where there were no 'just add water' solutions to difficult problems, both personal and social. These communities would be places of safety and fun, where people knew that in many ways 'all you need is less', places of environmental sensitivity and care for creation, gatherings where no questions are out of bounds. They would be places where you could boil over with life or howl with anguish, because there was freedom and space for your humanity to be both released and supported. They would be well-watered oases in our spiritual deserts but also places of healing in the crazy consumer playground of modern life. These places and gatherings would be curators of creativity, and above all they would be communities of a love that gave no reasons and asked for no reply. I like to think of a church as a place where lives are lived generously, freely, undefended and full of laughter. Laughter is surely one of the characteristic sounds of the kingdom of God. When the people of God laugh, the kingdom of God is just around the corner.

It's all very well to write fine-sounding phrases, but no church leader can 'turn on' this kind of church with the flick of a strategic plan. Such churches grow from their Source. They're connected to the love that wouldn't let Jesus go, even though on the evening of Good Friday it looked as if all was lost. On Easter Day, the wires hummed again and Jesus rose up as never before. Only that Spirit of resurrection-life can create a new Church. The bad news is that the old Church might have to die first, or at least, many aspects of it might. Death and resurrection go together – or hadn't we noticed?

There are many books on the renewal of the Church. This isn't one of them. I'm simply suggesting that one of the consequences of the resurrection is that the Church needs to take on the character of Christ, and that means studying it very closely, and being prepared for whatever deaths are necessary in order to 'gain Christ' (Philippians 3.8). The Church will only ever be in draft form because it only has a provisional role in paving the way for the kingdom of God. But a humble and obedient Church, modelled on Jesus Christ, is one that God can raise from the dead. The wounds would remain, as they did on the risen body of Jesus, but the Body of Christ (the Church) would glow in the dark and be a beacon of hope for a bewildered culture.

In this chapter I've simply given examples of the kind of implications that the resurrection brings in its wake. But whether we take those implications seriously depends on how much confidence we put in the resurrection as the irreducible, burning core of our faith.

There's a much-quoted story, a true one, about that abiding passion. Three years after the Russian Revolution of 1917, a major atheist rally was arranged in Kiev. A powerful orator by the name of Bukharin was sent from Moscow, and for an hour he laid into the Christian faith with argument, abuse and ridicule. At the end there was silence. Then questions were invited. A man rose to speak. He was a priest from the Russian Orthodox Church. He turned to face the people and spoke just three words, the ancient liturgical greeting used at Easter. 'Christ is risen,' he declared solemnly. Immediately the entire assembly stood and gave the joyful response 'He is risen indeed. Alleluia!'

Bukharin could say nothing.

# 11

## *The leaver who remained: what happened?*

And then, suddenly, Jesus was no longer with them. He was absent, no longer appearing unnervingly at odd moments. He had gone. We call it the Ascension.

Come back with me to the footprint in the stone with which we started this book. Confusingly, we're in a small mosque at the top of the Mount of Olives. In the fourth century, Poimenia, a member of the imperial family, had a small courtyard chapel built here, open to the sky. The twelfth-century Crusaders replaced this with an octagon shrine surrounded by a monastery, but Saladin took that over in 1198 and a roof was constructed over the chapel as it became a mosque. It remains in Muslim hands, although Christian pilgrims are made welcome.

So here we are, gazing at a footprint in a stone, wondering how to respond to such a blatantly physical representation of an event that's essentially and inevitably beyond normal language to describe. What happened? And did it happen here? Only Luke records this strange experience. It's usually assumed that Matthew's account of Jesus commissioning his disciples in Galilee at the end of his Gospel is his record of the Ascension, but there's nothing actually in those verses of Matthew to say that Jesus was now departing to be with his Father. So let's stay with Luke, and he said it was on the Mount of Olives, a sabbath's day journey (2,000 paces) from the city, that this mysterious event happened.

But what happened? It's easier to say what didn't happen. Jesus didn't take off like a rocket and return to a distant heaven not yet discovered by cosmologists. When we see sandals sticking out of fluffy clouds at the top of a medieval painting we don't think this is what the Archbishop of Canterbury and the Regius Professor of Divinity at Oxford believe actually happened on some Judean hilltop long ago. Nor did the great theologians of the early Church necessarily think of heaven in a literalistic way.

> In the fourth century Athanasius said that 'When Christ sat on the right hand of the Father, he did not put the Father on his left.' In other words, to say with the Apostles Creed that 'He ascended into heaven and is seated at the right hand of the Father' is to make a theological point rather than a geographical one.[1]

When the Hebrew mind used spatial images it often meant something about spiritual rather than physical space.

You would have thought that for Mary and the baffled disciples the loss of Jesus, even of his intermittent presence after the resurrection, would have been heartbreaking. But no. They 'returned to Jerusalem with great joy; and they were continually in the temple blessing God' (Luke 24.52–53). They somehow knew that this was just the next scene in the Great Play, and they could trust the divine Playwright.

It was the end of the honeymoon of the resurrection period. The disciples had been living with excitement and frustration for nearly six weeks. They'd met Jesus in the garden, in their upper room and out on the road. They'd been up-country, fishing like the old days around Galilee, and they'd had a barbecue breakfast with him by the lake. Peter had had a special talk with Jesus about times past and responsibilities to come. Jesus had just kept popping up – and then disappearing for days on end.

But now all that had come to an end. John records Jesus predicting this moment. 'I am going to the Father and you will see me no longer' (John 16.10). They knew that Jesus would no longer be around as he had been because, as C. S. Lewis observed, 'a phantom can just fade away; but an objective entity must go somewhere – something must happen to it.'[2] And it had. The Ascension event affirms that Jesus' body did go somewhere. It went to the Father.

But even to say that is to realize that we are in completely uncharted territory with the resurrection body and the

Ascension experience. What Paul calls the 'spiritual body' is both continuous and discontinuous with bodies as we know them, but we would be wise not to limit the possibilities of God's action. After all, even in our current understanding of the physical universe, we know that carbon can exist in the incredibly hard form of a diamond or the soft, crumbly form of graphite. And in a quantum universe where everything is made up of infinitesimally small particles zooming around in empty space, who knows what the possibilities are? This is one of those times when we must simply let God be God and not try to pin down the bird of heaven.

So Jesus had left and the disciples knew it. It doesn't matter whether we imagine Jesus disappearing in the mist or suddenly not being there, as had happened in the upper room and on the road to Emmaus. Jesus would no longer be with them in the old/new way, and the only forwarding address was 'the Father'.

There's another spot where the Ascension is celebrated on the Mount of Olives. It's the Russian Orthodox Church of the Ascension just a short distance away from the humble Muslim mosque. Appropriately enough, the church isn't accessible to the ordinary non-Russian pilgrim, just as the Ascension, in its mysterious power, isn't easily accessible to any of us. It's strangely appropriate that we don't know where to celebrate the event. We could go to the mosque with the footprint – but we can't pray there in a Muslim shrine. We could try to find the cave on the Mount of Olives where Christians venerated the Ascension until Poimenia's open courtyard was built. (The Spanish nun Egeria records taking part in a celebration on a nearby hillock in 384.) Or we could wander off to Galilee, obeying the Easter angels who told the disciples to meet Jesus there, and we could imagine that Matthew's Great Commission was Jesus' farewell speech, up there in Galilee. The truth is, we don't know where to locate whatever happened, and that's somehow appropriate, because we don't know quite what happened or where. It's too mysterious. It's a one-off.

But we do know this. The Ascension clears the decks; it sorts out who's supposed to be where and doing what. The glory days of Jesus' personal ministry are in the past and the baton has passed to the apostles. Let's get down to work.

# 12

## The leaver who remained: what does it mean?

I once saw a performance by the Reduced Shakespeare Company of *The Bible: The Complete Word of God (abridged)*. It was full of wonderful light humour but when they came to the cross, resurrection and Ascension, they just told it straight. Towards the end, an actor simply stood on stage and said: 'And then Jesus ascended into heaven and sat at the right hand of the Father. And he will come again in glory to judge both the living and the dead, and his kingdom will have no end.' There was a pause, and then he said: 'That's pretty cool.' And then the show went on.

Indeed it is pretty cool. The Ascension may be a shadowy event in the Christian story but it casts a very long shadow. So what have Christian people made of this major feast that we always somehow lose in a midweek Communion service?

### The hero has returned home

There had to be an ending. The weeks of the resurrection appearances were wonderful but vaguely unreal. It was exciting to have Jesus appearing in unexpected places and then not being seen for days on end, and it kept you on your toes, but it couldn't go on for ever. And now they knew. This was a departure, an ending, a returning, a completion. In the poetic language which is all we have here, Jesus returned to his Father. The hero had returned home; the champion had gone back for the great welcome party and the tour of heaven in the open-top bus. He now drinks the wine of heaven rather than the vinegar of Calvary.

Language fails here, of course. Already we're using metaphors. It's like a toddler trying to describe passionate love. It's outside her world of reference. So too with us and the Ascension. We blunder around with the few letters of the divine alphabet that we've managed to learn, and hope that they'll convey something of the glory of the event. We speak of Jesus being Lord, King, sitting at the right hand of the Father, Christ interceding for us. We speak of Christ in glory, in splendour, 'on his throne'. We might even get a glimpse of what this means from some of our own language – we speak of being 'on cloud nine', feeling 'on top of the world', being 'high' on some great experience. These are clues, but they can't claim to be literal descriptions, or even half-adequate, in expressing the reality behind them. They're just the best we've got. So let's simply say that Jesus has 'ascended into heaven', and is seated at 'the right hand of the Father'. He's returned home.

The huge journey of the incarnation has come full circle and Jesus has done what God wanted him to do. The ministry was thrilling and demanding, the cross was hard and bitter agony, the resurrection was a complete delight, and then there was the joyful departure. Job done, surely? Well, no, but we'll look at that later. For now, we celebrate the hero's return.

## Jesus is Lord, and we're not

We've seen how the disciples went back to Jerusalem full of joy in spite of having lost the 'bodily' presence of their fantastic friend. Somehow they knew that it was all right, deeply all right. Jesus had been put in his place and so had they, and actually that was fine. The decks were cleared, the job descriptions worked out; time to get on with it. So they went back to Jerusalem full of anticipation and excitement.

It's good that Jesus is in his place. In him God has visited his people – but his place is in heaven. We have been visited, marvellously, and everything is different – but our place is on earth. The writer of Ecclesiastes puts it perfectly, 'God is in heaven, and you upon earth; therefore let your words be few' (Ecclesiastes 5.2). So all our attempts to play God ourselves, to go way beyond our brief and confuse ourselves with the Saviour, are torn down. I have a sign on my study door that says, 'Grandad: the Man, the Myth, the Legend.' I don't believe it, and nor does my family.

It's always been hard for us to know our limits. We're always building our towers of Babel, trying to storm the heavens and become like gods. We always imagine we could run the world better than God, so, as the German theologian Dietrich Bonhoeffer said, we edge him out of the world and on to a cross. We try to overturn the divine order ('God is in heaven and you upon earth') and to take over the reins of power. We see everything as our own show, with us as the stars. But the Ascension doesn't let us get away with this fantasy. It puts us in our place because it puts Jesus in *his* place. And Jesus is Lord.

That was the fundamental conviction of the early Church, that Jesus is Lord. That was what enabled them to stand firm when they were persecuted to death for refusing to acknowledge that Caesar was Lord. It was a huge price to pay for the central tenet of their faith, but they paid it because Jesus is Lord. Christians say the same today: Jesus is Lord and the Prime Minister isn't. Nor is the President of the United States, nor the City, nor big business, nor the media, nor Silicon Valley. Only Jesus. Our calling is to give substance to what that means day by day in our own particular spheres of influence. Sadly we have to admit that we often pretend to be married to God while having a secret affair with the world. Accepting the reality of Jesus as lord of my values, habits and temptations is easier said than done. Happily, through the incarnation and the Spirit (more later), there's now a ladder set up between heaven and earth, so we have the offer of unlimited help in our calling. The task is simply to proclaim by our life, words and actions that not only is Jesus *our* Lord, but we believe he is Lord of all.

## Humanity is given its true value

While the Ascension makes clear that Jesus is Lord and we are not, it nevertheless demonstrates that we have an extraordinary place in the annals of heaven and earth. In the Ascension Jesus takes humanity to the right hand of God. One of our own has a throne in heaven. Think how wonderful it was for the Argentinian people when one of their own became Pope. When

Francis took the chair of St Peter it was a huge affirmation for Argentinians. So it is for us, with Jesus exalted to the right hand of the Father. We've already seen how humanity was given new value as God entrusted himself to human flesh in the incarnation. We saw that value reaffirmed as God loved us enough to die for us. But now we see that human nature is taken into heaven, the very realm of God.

We often excuse ourselves by saying, 'Well, I'm only human.' As I write, tales of sexual harassment and abuse in the film industry, in Parliament, in business life and elsewhere are swirling around in the news, and you can almost hear the unspoken weasel words, 'I'm sorry, I'm only human.' That simply won't do. If we are truly human then we are most like God, and this has ethical implications. Any insult to the humanity of anyone, be they prince or pauper, Peruvian or Parisian, is strictly speaking blasphemy; God is insulted because God has given humanity its true value and taken it into the heartland of heaven.

The younger daughter of American diplomat William Howard Taft III once announced: 'My great-grandfather was President of the United States, my grandfather was Senator of Ohio, my father is Ambassador to Ireland, and I am a Brownie.' She knew her identity and was proud of it. So we too can be proud of our identity and that humanity has been given its true value at the right hand of God.

## Jesus is present, not absent

The danger of giving these chapters on the Ascension the title 'The leaver' is that we might actually believe it. Through the Ascension, Christ leaves our normal configurations of space-time, in order to be present for ever to anyone who wants that grace and favour. He was a leaver precisely in order to remain. Mary Magdalene tried to cling to Jesus in the resurrection garden, longing to re-establish her special relationship with him, but Jesus wouldn't let her do so. He had to move beyond being present to one set of people in one place and time, in order that he could be available to every set of people, everywhere, and throughout time. First, Jesus had to become the leaver; then he would become the remainer, the ever-present Christ. His last great promise in Matthew's Gospel is, 'Remember, I am with you always, to the end of the age' (Matthew 28.20).

The Ascension is about presence, not absence. 'God doesn't know how to be absent', said Martin Laird.[1] The problem is that *we* know all too well how to be absent, and how to miss the presence of God altogether. There's a vast desert in China where people can easily get lost and die from the heat and the absence of water. Dehydration has killed large numbers of the reckless and unprepared. Recently, however, an enormous reservoir of water has been discovered, lying just beneath the desert, bigger than the size of the five Great Lakes of North America combined. The tragedy is that so many people have died in that desert when such life-giving resources were lying so close. So it is with humankind. The presence of God is so close, just a heartbeat or a prayer away, but either we don't know that, or we don't want to know.

It's good to recognize special places that, for us, resonate with the divine. There's a cave in the hillside just above the traditional site of Jesus' resurrection breakfast by the Sea of Galilee, where Peter was put back together after his repeated denials of his Lord. It's a quiet spot if you choose the right time, after the morning coaches have left the Church of St Peter's Primacy. The cave is perhaps ten feet wide by five feet in height, and you're almost guaranteed to find it empty. It's an easy scramble from the road and gives inspiring views over Galilee. I love to go there to think and pray, to drink in the beauty and give my imagination free rein. It may well have been one of the places where Jesus himself went to pray, being less than a mile from Capernaum and at the foot of the Mount of Beatitudes, where 'while it was still very dark, he got up and went out to a deserted place' to pray (Mark 1.35). I imagine Jesus climbing up the starlit hills – just peace and silence and the path beneath his feet. It certainly feels like a place 'where Jesus knelt to share with thee, the silence of eternity', in the words of John Greenleaf Whittier's hymn. Some places just breathe the presence of God. It's good to identify our own special places.

Jesus is present, not absent, and the joy of every believer is to discover more of that presence, focused on Christ, made possible by the Ascension, and released through the Spirit. Jesus has gone up but he hasn't gone away spiritually. Yes, he's gone physically, but now the Spirit of Christ is available for all time. 'It is to your advantage that I go away, for if I do not go away, the Advocate will not come to you; but if I go, I will send him to you' (John 16.7).

## 'He's got the whole world in his hands'

In the Ascension we say that Christ has taken the supreme place alongside his Father, and that sovereignty belongs to him. In other words, 'He's got the whole world in his hands.' We used to sing it at the toddler group, complete with the exaggerated circle of the arms and the long drawn out 'whooole' world. It was fun as an action song but often left me feeling ambivalent about it as a theological statement, as my eyes swept round the parents and carers who sang along too. Could they believe it? Could I? Bill Bryson writes of an incident in Durham when he was walking across a bridge and felt a strange compulsion to look down to the river, and there to his horror he saw a child on the bank tumbling into the water and about to be carried away by the current. He shouted out and the mother rushed to the rescue, plucking the little boy out of the water just in time. Bryson says:

> I am not a religious soul, but I must say it does seem a little uncanny that on that morning of all mornings I should have looked over the bridge at such a propitious moment. I mentioned the story at lunch to one of the members of the cathedral, and he nodded sagely and pointed a finger heavenward, as if to say, 'It was God, of course.' I nodded and didn't say anything, but thought: 'Then why did He push him in?'[2]

Precisely. What does it mean to say, 'He's got the whole world in his hands'?

Jesus is Lord. Yes, but not Lord in the way the world often imagines lordship to be. This isn't lordship of the 'I'm in control and can intervene when I like' variety. This is lordship, the holding of God's world in his hands, through the only energy that's ultimately effective and lasting, and that's the universal energy of love. Perhaps this becomes clearer if we switch the image from 'lordship' to its close cousin, 'kingship'. One sort of kingship is the *absolute monarch*, what you might call the 'king of clubs', thrusting his decisions on his subjects, using force if necessary. Some people can only think of God in this distant, demanding, controlling kind of way. You meet it in phrases such as, 'He must have done something terrible to deserve that,' or 'We'd better have our baby christened just in case.' In case of what? In case God doesn't like babies who haven't been baptized? The kind of God we're offered in this king of clubs is one who's arbitrary and potentially vengeful – nothing like the Jesus we see in the Gospels.

Another image of kingship is the *ceremonial monarch*, the playboy prince, the pampered princess, the monarch you roll out to impress visitors – a kind of 'king of diamonds'. If Christ is this kind of king then the cross easily becomes just a piece of jewellery, and Easter an excuse for chocolate. Religion is fancy wrapping paper, carols from King's, the all-frills church wedding, bishops in pointy hats. Not remotely the ascended Christ.

Yet another image of kingship is that of the *constitutional monarch*, a working monarch, a 'king of spades' who gets his hands dirty and works hard, but is kept in place by a whole system of constitutional checks and balances. But since when could we put checks and balances on the freedom of God? How could Christ be a constitutional monarch trapped in the conventions of religion and social acceptability?

The image of kingship that fits, of course, is the *servant monarch* – the 'king of hearts'. This king loves and respects his people and desires only their good. He's there to listen and serve. He shares our journey, knows our needs. It's easy to see him entering the world by the back door, washing feet, and taking on the forces of dark despair. This is our God, the servant king, the king of hearts.

Ultimately only this form of lordship can hold and heal the world. This kind of lord only works from the inside out, not dipping into the pool of human mistakes and misery to sort things out when they've gone too far. God 'under-rules' in this world rather than 'over-rules'. But we can be absolutely sure that God will do everything that love can do, always. God is always on our side, always committed to our well-being. Julian of Norwich reflected on being seriously ill as a young woman in her *Revelations of Divine Love*:

> Do you wish to understand your Lord's meaning? Understand truly: love was his meaning. Who revealed it to you? Love. What did he show you? Love. Why did he show it? For love. Hold firmly to this and you will learn and know more of this.[3]

He's got the whole world in his hands, *if we see God working always and everywhere through love*. The picture I often have of that patient process is a mountain stream, bouncing its way joyfully down the hillside, sparkling in the sunlight, until it hits a blockage – rocks, branches, foliage. But it's not put off. It can't go straight on but it will inevitably find a way, over, under, round, whatever it takes. On goes the stream, larger now and joined by others. It dances down until it comes across a larger problem, a small landslip, more rocks, bigger debris from the forest. Again, the stream isn't defeated. It always finds a way, over, under, round, whatever it takes. And so the stream continues on its way, overcoming every obstacle, until eventually it empties into the big river that makes its majestic, unstoppable journey to the sea. Such are the ways of God. Love is never defeated; it just finds another way – over, under, round, whatever it takes. Love will always get through because it's ultimately irresistible.

John V. Taylor puts it like this: 'The truth about God is not so much that he is omnipotent as that he is *inexhaustible*. And for that reason he will always succeed.'[4] It's the inexhaustibility of God's love that eventually overcomes everything that stands in its way. But it might take a lifetime and more. It might take eternity.

# 13

## *The leaver who remained: what does it mean for us now?*

We know how to celebrate Christmas, even if we bury the treasure under a thousand distractions. We know how to celebrate Easter, although society tries to tame it with spring flowers and chocolate. But sadly we don't really know how to celebrate Ascension. It's buried in a midweek evening service and doesn't get the glory of its more exalted cousins.

There was a time in my life when I had to give the Ascension the attention it's due. The Archdeacon of Canterbury had by ancient statute to preach at the Ascension Day Eucharist in the cathedral. I only held that office for five years but I know that each year I found myself caught between wanting to do justice to this great festival and avoiding saying the same thing every time. But it did at least set me thinking about the implications of the Ascension for our daily discipleship.

### We have a friend in high places

It's not that we want to pull strings; it's just that 'we have a great high priest who has passed through the heavens', and he isn't 'a high priest unable to sympathize with our weaknesses, but . . . one who in every respect has been tested as we are, yet without sin' (Hebrews 4.14–15). That's very good news. We have a friend who truly understands, and that friend is in a position to do something about it. Imagine you have cancer and your doctor says that she's been through this kind of cancer too. Imagine your son has been in trouble with the police and your lawyer says that he's had a similar situation with his own son as well. Imagine you've been trying to sort out a housing dispute and your MP says that she was in that very position a few years ago.

It's very reassuring. And now that doctor, that lawyer, that MP is working flat out to help you.

So it is with the exalted Jesus. He works flat out for us in the halls of heaven, and that gives us confidence to approach God in our prayers with complete honesty and a large measure of hope. 'Let us therefore approach the throne of grace with boldness, so that we may receive mercy and find grace to help in time of need' (Hebrews 4.16). It's not pulling strings, and nor is it favouritism, because Jesus is the friend of all sinners, all of us, and acts on behalf of everyone. Even better, the Father who hears our prayers is completely at one with the Son in wanting to make things work out. With his scarred hands and wounded side Jesus says to the heavenly host, 'Well, you see, it's like this . . .' Because he knows. He's been there. He's been tested as we are. He's been in the thick of battle and knows the struggles that we all have. And he's completely on our side – the Advocate.

The life, death and new life of Jesus has made all the difference. When Jesus left his followers in that mysterious event we call the Ascension, it wasn't just a return to the bad old days. People used to say, 'God is in heaven, but we're always stuck here. We wish to goodness he'd just come and have a look for himself and send a messiah to sort things out.' But now he's actually been. And he hasn't just looked, he's entered. His star has blazed through the Palestinian sky and come to earth. He's shown the way by being the Way; he's taught the truth by being the Truth; he's demonstrated the life by being the Life. And more than anything, he's taken the mess and misery of the world upon himself and drawn the terrible sting out of it. He's been crucified and risen. So heaven has broken into earth, and earth has been taken up into heaven.

This is what lies behind those evocative words, 'It is Christ Jesus, who died, yes, who was raised, who is at the right hand of God, who indeed intercedes for us' (Romans 8.34). We do indeed have a friend in high places.

There's one other aspect of all this that we need to note. It's quite possible that the emphasis on the 'high places' could distance us from Jesus rather than draw us closer to God. We might feel very much at home with the earthy Jesus of the incarnation, the man who knew all about the price of fish and how to protect a flock of sheep, who touched lepers and went to supper with society's rejects. But now we have Jesus ascended, glorified. Now we have a Lord of blazing holiness and unapproachable light. Now we have Jesus who has become the eternal Christ and sits in judgement on the world. Is he just too glorified?

This was the problem Geoffrey Howard wrote about in his beautiful little book *Dare to Break Bread*. And his answer – as it were from God – was this:

> Geoff, the sun is ninety-three million miles away. If you get much nearer to it, you will be incinerated, but that doesn't stop you enjoying the sunshine. My ascended glory is a bit like that. It is awesome. And yet, you catch no more than an inkling of it in the Sanctus. Surely you can sing of my glory from afar and appreciate me as you appreciate the sun on a spring day? That's not too dazzling. I do not want to frighten you with my presence. Why do you think I choose to meet you in bread and wine?[1]

The ascended Christ could seem awesome and unapproachable, but that's precisely the point of using the image of 'the friend in high places'. He is a friend as well as a king. Heaven and earth have been joined. The ladder that Jacob saw in a dream (Genesis 28.10–22), with angels ascending and descending between earth and heaven, has become a reality in the incarnation, and Jesus is the interpreter between the two, equally at home in both. We can claim 'What a Friend we have in Jesus', and also resolve to 'Crown him with many crowns, the Lamb upon his throne.'

## We have a clear job description

There's an old legend that tells of Jesus returning home in the Ascension and encountering two archangels wandering past on their way to harp practice. They ask Jesus how it went. 'It was tough,' said Jesus, 'wonderful but tough, particularly at the end.' 'So how have you left things?' they asked. 'Oh, it's fine,' replied Jesus. 'I've left Peter, James and John and the others to get on with the job. They're a great team.' 'You must be joking,' said the archangels, genuinely shocked. 'That crowd of failures who were always messing up and in the end either denied you or ran away! You cannot be serious.' 'Well,' said Jesus, 'I have no other plans.'

Nor has he. We are the ones charged with the task of announcing and bringing in the kingdom. There's no plan B. Jesus' method was to work himself out of a job and hand it over to us. Matthew records Jesus telling his followers to go and make all nations his disciples, baptizing them and teaching them everything that Jesus had commanded. 'And what shall we do on Tuesday . . .?' they might have asked, ironically. This was a huge task, to change gear from a Palestinian ministry to a worldwide project. But they weren't dismayed. This was a task worth living and dying for, to 'proclaim release to the captives and recovery of sight to the blind, to let the oppressed go free, to proclaim the year of the Lord's favour' (Luke 4.18–19). There were other parts of the job description too: feed the hungry, give drink to the thirsty, welcome the stranger, clothe the naked, visit the sick and the prisoner and indeed anyone in need. And what made these commands all the more pressing was that by doing these things they would be doing them for Jesus himself (Matthew 25.35ff.).

Of course the task of building the kingdom of God is overwhelming, even for those who've seen Jesus at work at close quarters. So what we have to do is simply put up flags of ownership over small parts of the building site – this wonderful wreckage of Eden – wherever we can do good. Every act of love and grace in a world where the big ones are always eating the little ones, and where it often seems that nations are besotted with violence, is a victory for the kingdom. And I do mean *every* act of love. Throughout the ministry of Jesus we see how he takes small things as the key to abundance – the mustard seed that becomes a six-foot plant, the empty water jars that overflow with gallons of fine wine, the seed lavishly thrown about the field that yields a hundred-fold, the five loaves and two fish that result in twelve baskets full of leftovers, the bread and wine that grows a worldwide Church.

'Think small, dream big' seems to have been Jesus' mantra. Do whatever is before you, and build the kingdom piece by loving piece. So the smile, the wave, the cup of tea, the visit to a new resident down the road, the hour spent with an alienated teenager, joining a credit union, writing a letter for a political prisoner, committing two hours a week to the Samaritans or the food bank – all these are seeds for Jesus to use and multiply, or (remembering his actions when feeding the five thousand) to take, bless, break open and give away, as he does and as we do at every Communion. Our task is to respond with love and generosity to the situation before us; God's task is to scale up the effect. Love gives the ground plan, the building materials, the skill and the motivation to build the kingdom – and not a love that's all fluffy pink mist and good intentions. What's needed is love with steel at the centre: a love that gives food to the hungry even when they're ungrateful, that welcomes the stranger even when he leaves with the family silver, that visits the prisoner even when his crime disgusts you, that clothes the naked even when his fashion sense is off the wall.

I'm suggesting that all of this is an overflow of the Ascension. The connection may not be obvious to the average Christian. But let's remember the experience of the disciples that day and thereafter. They weren't downhearted by the departure of their Lord; they returned to the city in high spirits because they knew it was now over to them. Jesus had cleared the decks and handed over the kingdom project to them, so everything they were to do now would be a result of being set free by the Ascension and empowered by the Spirit (see the next chapter). And so it is with us. Where the world sighs with sorrow, bleeds with injustice, or just needs loving, Christians will be there; they always are. We know only too well the ragged beauty of our own lives and how the presence of God ransoms, heals, restores and forgives; so what we know, we share.

Our confidence lies in the ascended Lord, and what he did with a random bunch of Middle Eastern youngsters who went down a mountain and set about changing the world.

## Before the ascended Christ we're often left speechless

There was a notice in an Austrian ski-lodge that read: 'Not to perambulate the corridors in the hours of repose in the boots of ascension.' You can see what they meant, but it's the old problem of language again. Translation is fraught with danger. Indeed, sometimes all language crumbles in the face of realities so profound that no words could even approach being adequate. The deepest human experiences often require silence – with the dying and bereaved, before a scene in nature that takes your breath away, when working hard or thinking deeply, when concentrating on writing or painting or solving a problem. And particularly when praying.

Coming before the majesty of God, glimpsing the glory of the ascended Lord, could and should leave us speechless. Whatever we say would be an incoherent babble, a 'noisy gong or a clanging cymbal'. Words should retire, slip away embarrassed. They may help us on the lower slopes, but when we get to the mountain-tops they need to hide in the rucksack until called for. Prayer usually starts in stillness and ends in silence. Indeed, if we're serious about God, I think we'll find, ultimately, that some words are indeed useful, but not very many. Sometimes it may come down to just one or two – 'Jesus', 'Before, you Lord', 'Come, Holy Spirit'. Silence is often the most straightforward and spacious way of encountering God because not too much of 'me' gets in the way.

When I led a group on a pilgrimage through the Sinai desert a few years ago we spent the first two hours each day walking in silence. All agreed it was the most profound time of the day. The fierce majesty of the desert and the near presence of the risen, ascended Lord were a very powerful combination, and could be savoured fully only in silence. At night we simply unrolled our sleeping bags and settled ourselves against some friendly rocks. We could then gaze at the dark infinity above us, awed at the billions of stars flung joyfully across space. Everything was alive with the exalted, cosmic Christ. Only silence could do justice to such profligate beauty.

But this exalted Lord is also nearby. Earth is saturated with heaven, and the heavenly Christ can be encountered in our own reality. Jesus was often pointing out that heaven isn't just a promise for the future but a gift for the present; it starts now, if we will but accept the nearness of the kingdom. Mark says that the essence of Jesus' message was that 'the time is fulfilled, and the kingdom of heaven has come near' (Mark 1.14). Now.

But how do we encounter Jesus and the kingdom in the rush and tumble of everyday life?

There are five particular practices that help me to discern the presence of Christ in the silence beyond our habitual prayers and liturgies. There's much more to prayer than this, but here we're thinking about the times when words just don't seem to be enough.

One way of praying is through *looking more closely at nature.* How often do we pass by the beauty of a garden, a park, a view through the car window, with scarcely a nod of acknowledgement? The conductor and composer Leonard Bernstein said that a great artist leaves us with the feeling that something is right with the world (although, of course, we also know that great art can show in penetrating ways what's out of joint in our world too). The works of the Great Artist show us how glorious the world is. If we train ourselves to walk more slowly through the natural world we have a feast of treats in store – the light funnelling through the trees, the innumerable shades of green, the variety of shapes and textures of the leaves, the astonishing intricacy in a flower-head, the birds singing their hearts out. You don't need to hug a tree, though it might help. And occasionally it will take your breath away. I was driving on the section of the M6 that goes through the eastern Lake District and I encountered ('saw' is too weak a word) a fellside of exquisite contours, drenched in light, that was so stunningly beautiful it was genuinely painful. I could hardly contain the onrush of beauty, the ravishing of my senses. It was an extreme example of what is available to us daily as we train ourselves to notice what God has provided abundantly, and at no cost. For example, it can be a deeply refreshing experience to spend 15 minutes with a square yard of God's good earth – particularly if it's by the water's edge or a stream. If we spend time simply observing the wonderful variety of colours, shades, textures, movements, patterns, insects, webs, reflections of light, and so forth, we can be brought to a deep respect and reverence for all this intricate life before us, and taken into prayer.

*Lectio divina,* or holy reading, is a second method of encountering the God who invites us into silence, this time in a passage of Scripture. Rather than simply finding out what's in that passage – which we probably know anyway – it allows us to munch the Word of God thoughtfully, to get 'up close and personal' with it. The process has three stages – reading, reflecting and responding (with an optional resting). We first read a passage from the Gospels twice, slowly, and see which word or phrase pops up and asks for attention (reading). Then we chew the word or phrase, slowly, patiently, thoughtfully, to get all the meaning and goodness we can out of it, looking at it this way and that, letting it resonate with our own experience (reflecting). Then we pray out of those ruminations in whatever way our reflections have taken us (responding). I rarely come away from *lectio divina* disappointed. God makes himself present. In the Gospels Jesus stands very near.

A third way of encountering God beyond words is through *Ignatian meditation*, which engages with a Gospel passage through the senses. Here we read a passage of the Gospels carefully – again, it's best to do it twice. Then we put the Bible aside. What we want to do is to enter the story, encounter the characters, and hopefully meet with Jesus. So we become a participant and go slowly through the story, using our senses to do so. Imagine the feeding of the five thousand. *Sight*: What does the crowd look like? And what about Jesus and the disciples? What do you see? *Hearing*: Can you hear the waves, the birds? Who says what and how do they say it? *Feelings*: What does it feel like sitting there listening to Jesus? And what about the sun, the grass, the children playing? *Taste*: What does the bread taste like? And the salted fish? *Smell*: Can you smell the sea, the heat rising?

So you go through the story without rushing it, asking those kinds of questions. And maybe at the end you go and find Jesus himself. Sit with him, ask him about what has happened. Ask him how it might affect you. Ask him what you should do next. Then, when you're ready, or Jesus has to move on, leave the scene, gently and carefully. It would be surprising if after a few attempts at this way of praying you didn't discover much more about yourself and about Jesus.

A fourth way of encountering the presence of Christ in the everyday run of life (but without using words) is what the Jesuits call the *Examen*, a way of looking back and reflecting on the learning of the last day. Rather than letting the day be lost and forgotten, and rather than living unaware of the presence of God through that day, we give space for God to uncover the deeper movements of the Spirit. The simplest way I know of doing this is in four stages. First we ask God to reveal what there is to learn from the day. Second, we look for those times when we were grateful, when we felt most alive, connected, energized, aware of 'something more' going on. What was happening then? What was God showing us through that experience? Third, we go back and look for those times when we felt out of touch, unconnected, lifeless, diminished, anything but grateful. What was going on there? What can we learn about ourselves from that experience? Last, we put the next 24 hours into God's hands, and pray for an awareness of God's life-giving presence in what we say, think and do.

The fifth way of encountering God's presence when we've realized that words are crumbling into incoherence before the beauty of God is *contemplative or centring prayer*. The heart of this form of prayer is simply presenting ourselves before God without agenda, and letting God be God. So often our prayers and liturgies talk incessantly, words piled on words, and God can only politely look on. In centring prayer we strip away our defences and in the best sense 'get out of the way' and put God in the driving seat. We sit comfortably but alert. We consciously relax the body, particularly at its habitual points of stress such as the shoulders. We listen to noises off, notice them and put them aside. We notice our breathing, regular and life-giving. Then we name our prayer word ('Come, Holy Spirit', 'Jesus', 'Be still') like putting a feather down on a piece of cotton, as someone described it.

And that's it. We wait, we stay attentive, we repeat the prayer word when our thoughts wander off – as they will, many times. We're making ourselves available to God and it's entirely up to God what happens, which may well seem to be nothing. But it's never nothing to God, who will be present, loving, healing, filling, resting in us. It's not for us to judge the 'success' or otherwise of a time of centring prayer. It's all mutual gift in a language beyond words.

These are five quiet ways of encountering the reality of the divine, and so *experiencing* the presence of God rather than just *talking to* God – or even talking *at* God. Christ is ascended, certainly, but he hasn't left us. This is a 'leaver' who remained. Mary Magdalene was encouraged not to hold on to him, but only so that he could be present to her, and to us all, anywhere. But if we truly glimpse the scale and glory of the ascended Lord we may find that we're left speechless, and then, through different forms of silent prayer, come nearer to him than ever.

# 14

## *The promise: what happened?*

It was mid-morning and hot. We tumbled out of the coach, momentarily blinded by the light, and set off up the slope towards a room called the Cenacle (or 'dining room'), to which is attached a set of somewhat contentious traditions. But if we wanted to encounter the events around Pentecost here at least was a place to start. The coming of the Holy Spirit was a watershed moment and we wanted to stand near to where it might have happened. The Cenacle is an upper room above a tomb erroneously called the Tomb of David and near the beautiful Benedictine Church of the Dormition built in 1900 to commemorate the mother of Jesus 'falling asleep'. Certainly there's a strong tradition holding that this area of the upper city called Mount Zion (though not David's Mount Zion, which was lower down) was the base of the Jesus community and therefore a possible location for the Last Supper, the resurrection appearances and Pentecost. Scholarly opinion is reticent on the issue of location for all these events, but who knows?

We wanted to trace the event that gave birth to the Church and, failing anywhere better, we had come to the Cenacle. We trudged up the metal staircase to reach a spacious, airy room with high vaulted ceilings and gothic pillars. A pleasant room, certainly, but could this be the site of the revolution that changed the world?

In the fourth century the Emperor Theodosius built a small church here that was enlarged in the next century. Waves of invaders destroyed the building but it seems clear that early Christians in Jerusalem had identified this place as the site of Pentecost, and indeed a less reliable tradition associates it with the setting of the Last Supper as well. The current room probably dates from the fourteenth century so we were relying on early Christian memory rather than anything architectural. It was really a place to release the imagination.

We looked around. If not here, near here, or below here, one morning several weeks after the resurrection and a few days after Jesus had left them, an event occured that took the disciples' breath away – and gave them a new breath (the Hebrew word for breath also means spirit). Until now the disciples had been locked in a no-man's-land of wonder and bewilderment as Jesus had appeared and disappeared at seemingly random times and places. They were struggling to make sense of it all, both thrilled and puzzled. But now they were transformed.

In Acts 2, Luke describes a morning full of drama and intensity. As we've discussed before, language about transcendence is language pushed to breaking point. The best words that Luke could find for describing that morning were of a huge wind sweeping through the room and the disciples being so caught up in this extraordinary experience of the Spirit that it seemed as if fire was burning around them and they were speaking in other languages. There was a release of energy in that room that simply couldn't be contained. It attracted crowds of people who were living in Jerusalem but who came from all over the Middle East, and each one heard the disciples speaking in their own language. It was a crazy morning.

The key issue, however, was that from that moment the disciples knew what they had to do and they had the energy to do it. Not to put too fine a point on it, they knew that their task was to tell the nations – whatever the cost – that a new world had been born. Instead of being the frightened disciples of Good Friday or the exultant disciples of Easter Day or the worshipping disciples of Ascension Day, they were now the purposeful, Spirit-filled disciples of the Day of Pentecost. They were 'on fire' for Christ. Nothing would stop them now.

It's always been difficult for us to speak lucidly about the Day of Pentecost, even though the disciples clearly spoke with astonishing lucidity. Instead we've established traditions of *doing* rather than speaking. Different cultures have come up with a variety of ways of marking this most amazing day. Mark Oakley gives a very helpful run-down of some of them in his book *A Good Year*,[1] and I borrow unashamedly from him.

In England the day was known as Whitsun after the white clothes worn by those being baptized. I well remember the Whitsun walks in our parish, a procession through the streets that celebrated the Christian community getting out into the world. In some places horse racing happened that day too, with the horses representing the Spirit galloping through our lives and sweeping us on. In France one tradition was to blow trumpets during the service to represent the mighty wind that swept through the upper room and through the lives of the disciples. In Italy rose petals used to be scattered from the ceilings of churches to recall the fiery tongues of flame that appeared on the heads of the disciples. In Russia, flowers and green branches are still brought to church, representing the freshness of the Spirit.

My favourite tradition came from medieval Bavaria where a wooden dove, symbol of the Spirit, would be lowered through the church roof to hover over the congregation. What makes it particularly lovable, however, was that as the dove was lowered, choirboys up in the roof spaces would pour buckets of water over the congregation to literally drench them with the Spirit. What this did for church attendance that day is not recorded.

As we clambered back on the coach, gratefully taking a fresh bottle of cold water from the coach refrigerator, we couldn't be sure quite what we'd seen, or what precisely had happened on the Day of Pentecost, or where it had happened, but we were at least confirmed in the knowledge that without that world-changing event we wouldn't even have been there. On that day an explosion of power and joy had taken place, the effects of which are still spreading over the entire world.

But let's dig a bit deeper. What was really going on?

# 15

## *The promise: what does it mean?*

What do we make of the Holy Spirit? I know the question ought to be, 'What does the Holy Spirit make of us?' but the first question is quite a puzzle for many Christians. It recalls the conversation of a man leaving church one morning and saying, 'Thank you for that sermon, Vicar. I never did understand that topic. I still don't understand it – but at a higher level.'

Western art has also struggled with the Holy Spirit, often depicting the Trinity as two men and a bird. The bird, however, has much to commend it as an image of the Holy Spirit. Recalling the event when Jesus had been baptized by John, Luke says, 'the Holy Spirit descended on him in bodily form like a dove' (Luke 3.22). St Augustine and other early theologians were fond of saying, 'No dove, no Church': in other words, without the Holy Spirit the Church cannot exist.

There are so many themes to be pulled out of a theology of the Spirit; I'll focus on just a few.

### The Spirit makes Christ present in a new way

When Jesus disappointed Mary Magdalene in the Easter garden by pulling away from her touch, he was saying that in future he had to be present to her in a different way. This is it. He would be present to her, and to all who wanted, through his Spirit. It was the promise of John 16.7: 'It is to your advantage that I go away, for if I do not go away, the Advocate will not come to you; but if I go, I will send him to you.' Jesus gave a similar promise to the disciples just before his final departure: 'I am sending upon you what my Father promised; so stay here in the city until you have been clothed with power from on high' (Luke 24.49).

This Spirit that Jesus promised wasn't any old spirit, an impersonal, unrelational life-force; it was the Spirit of Jesus. Paul makes this clear in Romans 8.9 where he conflates our experience of God and of Jesus with our experience of the Spirit. 'You are not in the flesh; you are in *the Spirit*, since the *Spirit of God* dwells in you. Anyone who does not have the *Spirit of Christ* does not belong to him.' Spirit of God; Spirit of Jesus; Spirit – the experience is one and the same, or at least, one and similar.

One of the tasks of the Spirit is to point to Jesus. 'When the Advocate comes, whom I will send to you from the Father, the Spirit of truth who comes from the Father, he will testify on my behalf' (John 15.26). The image that verse suggests to me is of a floodlight pouring light on the subject (Jesus), yet being itself modest and undemonstrative. The floodlight doesn't want to be the object of scrutiny but rather to point to the thing (person) of beauty. The Spirit points to Christ.

When I first came to a faith for myself and not for my parents it was the figure of Jesus that fascinated and captivated me. This Jesus stepped off the thin pages of the New Testament and into the world of my own experience. Who takes the credit for that? I came to see that it was the Holy Spirit who made Jesus real, and who didn't need the limelight for him/herself. The Spirit's task was to make Christ real, to pour light on the living Jesus, and I gladly responded to the brilliance of the figure I now recognized as Lord.

## The Spirit empowers the life and mission of the Church

The new Jesus movement – soon to be called the Church – was powerless without the Holy Spirit. After the resurrection the disciples were like iron filings scattered about a workbench; when the magnet comes they instantly align with its magnetism and take on a new identity and purpose. When we consciously draw upon the energy of the Spirit and align ourselves with God's life, our own lives take on direction; we start to 'go with the flow' of divine energy that surges through all of life, if we will but recognize it.

Even then, this energy has to move beyond being a lot of theological or spiritual hot air. We can easily produce much spiritual steam without it being converted into power. The test of

Pentecost was never the wonderful feelings it generated, but always the effective power it produced in the lives of men and women driven out to be and to tell the Good News. The industrial revolution began when steam was harnessed into power that could drive engines. So it is with the life of the Church and of individual Christians. Feelings are fine, but release for the captives, recovery of sight for the blind and letting the oppressed go free is much more important.

Life in the Spirit, or empowered by the Spirit, then becomes the new normal. And being given gifts by the Spirit also comes with the territory (1 Corinthians 12.7–11). We are all given gifts, and therefore, like children who never come to a birthday party empty-handed, we all come to God's party with gifts to offer. We may be shy about producing the gifts but nothing is ever too little – and how it's wrapped is irrelevant. The best gifts often come from the most unlikely-looking sources. I constantly have to reprimand myself for making judgements about the skills or experience I imagine someone bringing. The unassuming elderly woman who turns out to know everyone in the community, to be in touch with everything that's going on, and to have wisdom to give for all situations. The quiet teenager who turns out to be a genius on IT and revolutionizes the church's communications. The busy professional woman who somehow makes time to visit people in need and mentor people in trouble. Not the 'wrapping' I expected, but gifts within of real authenticity and value.

It's easy to lament that we have been given *this* gift and not *that* one. I sometimes lament the fact that I seem to have helped so few people actually to come to faith. The gift of evangelism in me is obviously deeply hidden, and yet my primary motivation has always been to help people discover the joy of Christ. Gradually, however, I have come to accept that my gifts lie more in teaching and pastoral care, building people up in Christ rather than being the initiator of faith. 'The gifts he gave were that some would be apostles, some prophets, some evangelists, some pastors and teachers . . .' (Ephesians 4.11). I've come to accept that my gifts are those of 'pastor and teacher' – but I'll always want to give a reason for the hope that's in me.

## Everything has changed

The two themes above are significant enough – that Christ is present in a new way and that the Spirit empowers the life and mission of the Church. But a theology of the Spirit will make even greater claims. Everything has now changed. The world, the faith, and everything we do as believers is transformed by the coming of the Spirit. Rupert Shortt in *God Is No Thing* quotes Ignatius of Litakia, a leading Syrian Christian who at a conference of the World Assembly of Churches said this:

> Without the Holy Spirit, God is far away, Christ stays in the past, the Gospel is a dead letter, the Church is simply an organisation, authority simply a matter of domination, mission a matter of propaganda, liturgy no more than an evocation, Christian living a slave morality.
>
> But with the Holy Spirit, the cosmos is resurrected and groans with the birth-pangs of the Kingdom, the risen Christ is there, the Gospel is the power of life, the Church shows forth the life of the Trinity, authority is a liberating service, mission is a Pentecost, the liturgy is both memorial and anticipation, human action is deified.[1]

Those are very big claims. Did you notice 'the cosmos is resurrected and groans with the birth-pangs of the Kingdom'? That's the cumulative effect of the incarnation, the cross, the resurrection, the Ascension and Pentecost. All has been done; everything is in place for the revolution to begin. Indeed, it's already in progress and we have the privilege of getting into the slipstream of God's new creation, which Jesus code-named 'the kingdom of God', and there we add our energy to the enormous flow of God's divine life. We ally ourselves with any projects that resonate with the marks of the kingdom, resisting oppression, advocating for justice, working for reconciliation, lifting up the lowly and filling the hungry with good things (Luke 1.52–53).

Of course, this conviction that everything has changed doesn't immediately accord with our perception of how things are in the world. The story is told of a Jewish rabbi who was teaching a class of trainees. One of them asked: 'Rabbi, Christians say the

Messiah has already come. What do you say?' The rabbi went over to the window and looked down at the street for a while. Then he turned back to the class. 'It doesn't look much like it to me,' he said.

Nor does it. The world often seems to be overwhelmed with multiple darknesses. Christian faith, however, maintains that the kingdom of God is unstoppable. While the world strikes a succession of matches to mitigate the darkness, faith says that the dawn is irresistible and, if we will but see it, the dawn is starting to lift the darkness beyond the horizon and eventually it will flood the world with light. Yes, it's not empirically evidenced. It's a belief based on faith and hope, but those gifts are rooted in the story of God's decisive actions in the world, and in particular the five interventions that are the subject of this book. At its heart the world is not mad but sane, and its future rests ultimately in the hands of an inexhaustible Love.

## We are introduced to the third person of the Trinity

If speaking about the Holy Spirit is difficult, how on earth shall we make sense of the Trinity? We try, of course. In my time I've tried many simple formulas to explain the 'dream team' of Christianity. I've tried God in creation (the Father), God in history (the Son), God in us (the Spirit). God above, God beside, God within. I've tried creative love, rescuing love, indwelling love. I enjoy the poetic approach of Bishop David Jenkins, of God being greater than great, closer than close, more loving than love.

But I admit defeat. God is beyond our understanding and all language about God is therefore bound to be metaphorical – and inadequate. It's like a child in nursery learning her first few letters of the alphabet and being asked to explain quantum physics. Or the missionary in Africa in the mid-nineteenth century trying to explain what the engine of a train was like. He took two tree trunks and arranged them in parallel lines on the ground. He put a patient old cow between them and hung a steam kettle round her neck. 'That's like an engine,' he said. He could see they weren't impressed.

Nevertheless, it could also be said that the idea of the Trinity was the result of an outpouring of extraordinary intellectual energy in the early Church that produced this breakthrough in the human imagination. It's a bit like the energy going into computing at present, or artificial intelligence. The early Christians discovered the Trinity through the reality of their worship and the energy of their mission; attempts at definition came later.

Whatever the adequacy of the model, the third reality of God that early theologians needed to come to terms with was that of the Holy Spirit. God the Creator was well known. God the Son was the one who had overturned the tables of their religious thinking. But God the Holy Spirit was the one they now had to include in the Godly play of the Trinity.

If we are to do justice to the scale of the Holy Spirit in Christian thinking we have to break through the limitations of Trinitarian thinking about 'two men and a bird', or worse, 'two men and a spook'. The Spirit is not just a continuation of the life of Jesus, although Jesus bequeathed the Spirit to us. We have to dig deep into the life of God and see how the Spirit was active in Genesis where the Spirit of God hovered, or brooded, over the waters. The Spirit was the agent of creation, bringing the universe to birth, including humankind. But it isn't just this first creation for which the Spirit is responsible; it's also our re-creation after the resurrection. The Spirit gave new life to Jesus (Romans 8.11), and it's the Spirit who will give new life to us. God breathed life into the body of Adam, and Jesus breathed new life into his disciples (John 20.22: 'Receive the Holy Spirit'). So let's not domesticate the Spirit. The Spirit is the worthy, indeed necessary, third party of the Trinity.

This understanding of the scale of the Spirit's activity has been wonderfully explored in John V. Taylor's classic study *The Go-Between God*.[2] Earthed in the pervading normalities of everyday life and relationships, Taylor points to the presence and work of the Spirit in every facet of the activity of God and the life of creation. He demonstrates how the Holy Spirit is the director of the whole enterprise of the Church's mission. If we forget or minimize the work of the Spirit, we have removed the supporting structure of the Church's life.

These are stirring claims. But how do they work out now in our own discipleship?

# 16

## *The promise: what does it mean for us now?*

It's exhilarating to see the Spirit at work. I see the Spirit slipping through cracks in society's concrete when I go to Israel/Palestine, easing open the rigid positions in which people have become entombed, and offering grace and hope. I see it when I meet the Parents Circle, as mentioned previously. Two parents, one Jewish, one Palestinian, come to see us in Jerusalem to tell us how they work together in spite of both losing a child in the violence that simmers and sometimes explodes in Israel, the West Bank and Gaza. Their respect and care for each other is tangible. Their commitment to keep on telling their story is inspirational. We see the Spirit at work.

Another day we go out to the countryside southwest of Bethlehem in the Palestinian West Bank to meet an extraordinary family in the Tent of Nations. Constantly under pressure from the five Jewish Settlements surrounding them, they've been in court on and off for over 25 years to defend their right to the land, for which they have legal documentation. Their fruit and olive trees have been bulldozed, their roads blocked with concrete slabs, but still they say, 'We refuse to be enemies.' They host work parties of young people from their own country and abroad to encourage them in the ways of peace and reconciliation. The Spirit moves daily through that farm.

In Bethlehem itself there are many places of mercy. One such is the Holy Family Hospital, which has a fine reputation as a maternity hospital serving the West Bank. An orphanage called the St Vincent Crèche operates there too. We visit the orphanage, feeling somewhat voyeuristic, but are assured that the children love having visitors to talk to and play with them. There seems nothing more appropriate for Christians to be doing than bringing children safely to birth in Bethlehem, and caring for the victims of loss, prejudice and pain. The Spirit flows through the corridors of that hospital and the orphanage within it.

The Holy Spirit is much needed in the Holy Land. Fortunately, wherever there is need, the Spirit has got there first.

## The Spirit energizes God's people

Imagine a child receiving a beautifully wrapped Christmas present. He rips off the paper and there it is, the electronic toy he's been longing for. He dives into the box, pulls it out and switches it on. Nothing. He tries again. Nothing. Desperately he goes back into the box to see if he's missed something, and there he finds the instructions with that fatal little phrase: 'Batteries not included.' And it's Christmas Day, and the shops are shut.

Is that how God sees the Church sometimes – so much potential, but missing the power of the Holy Spirit? Do we sometimes try to go it alone, forgetting that we are designed to live and work in the flow of the Spirit? Personally, too, we may have felt that there's more in this Christian faith somewhere, but we're not quite sure where it is.

A nineteenth-century Christian leader called D. L. Moody realized that he had been trying to do everything through his own strength and wisdom, so he opened himself to the renewing energy of the Spirit. He said, 'All the time I'd been tugging and carrying water, but now I have a river that carries me.' It took a daunting experience of nervous exhaustion to convince me that I couldn't just carry on in my own sweet way, trusting in my abilities and the generosity of time. The Maker's instructions include the gift of the Maker too.

When Jesus came to Nazareth, as recorded in Luke 4, he quoted Isaiah 61:

> The Spirit of the Lord is upon me, because he has anointed me to bring good news to the poor. He has sent me to proclaim release to the captives and recovery of sight to the

blind, to let the oppressed go free, to proclaim the year of
the Lord's favour. (Luke 4.18)

Jesus claimed that experience of the Spirit's anointing as his
own. He laid out his manifesto and in the power of the Spirit
he set about fulfilling it through his ministry of liberation in
Galilee and beyond. No forgotten manifesto promises here.
Pope Francis has talked about the globalization of indifference
being a destructive illness that turns hearts to stone. What Jesus
offered and embodied was the heart of flesh that Ezekiel had
spoken of (Ezekiel 36.26), a heart that moved to the music of
the Spirit and met the needs of wounded, oppressed and anxious people wherever he encountered them.

What does that mean in our day? Michael Lloyd puts it
well:

> When we do our evangelism in such a way as to [include]
> those who couldn't or wouldn't read for pleasure, and those
> who feel awkward in a social setting, and those who feel
> educationally out of their depth, then we are remembering
> to *preach good news to the poor.* When we help run an Alpha
> course in prison or help support a prisoner when they are
> released, when we write our Amnesty International letters,
> or visit the housebound, or take a group of disadvantaged
> children to the beach, or run a Deaf Awareness course at
> our church, we are *proclaiming freedom for the prisoners.*
> When we pray for people's healing, or pay for someone
> to have a cataract operation in a Third World country . . .
> when we provide service sheets and hymn books and
> Bibles in Braille, when we offer to read for someone who
> is blind, we are proclaiming that *recovery of sight* is part of
> the Messianic agenda. When we write letters to our MPs
> about the injustices of world trade, when we buy fairly
> traded products, when we stand up for someone at work
> who has been unfairly treated, we are proclaiming that the
> Spirit will not rest until the *oppressed are released.*[1]

All this is the potential of the people of God as they open
themselves to the power and energy of the Spirit because, in

the Maker's instructions, batteries are definitely included – but they have to be inserted.

## The Spirit permeates all of life

When I listen to the second movement of a symphony the music usually comes down from the excitement of the first movement and offers instead serene melodies and quiet grandeur. Somehow this movement restores my soul; it fills me up. The disciples and the fast-growing early Church had a deep, calm confidence that enabled them to move out from Jerusalem and win hearts and minds, souls and bodies throughout the known world. When you read Paul's letters you get a picture of churches that are full of problems, certainly, but also full of hope, faith and Godly confidence. This is the second movement, full of faith, following the first movement which was full of the energy of Jesus and his mission.

And so it has been ever since. The ongoing life of the Holy Spirit, both in the Church and in the world, fills up every space that comes available. The Spirit is like a rising tide engulfing every nook and cranny of a coastline, not forcing any openings that aren't there, but filling abundantly any that are. The Spirit permeates all of life, and gives vigour and fullness to every person, institution and community, every part of creation to which the Spirit is welcome. The Spirit fills life with life.

You can see it in Jesus. John V. Taylor writes:

Christians say that the Spirit possessed the man Jesus Christ, making him the most aware and sensitive and open human being who has ever lived – ceaselessly aware of God so that he called him, almost casually, Father, and fantastically aware of every person who crossed his path, especially the ones no one else noticed.[2]

In other words, the Spirit filled Jesus with divine life. The possibility exists, therefore, that the Spirit can do the same for us, to the extent that we are open and receptive.

We live in the overflow of that divine life of the Spirit. And that only emphasizes again that the heart of our faith isn't rules, regulations and rituals but relationship. It's about experience before it's about proposition. Faith isn't static but dynamic; God is in the flow of the Spirit and we need to nurture our participation in that flow by the practice of prayer. Prayer is many things, but one image that can help us understand it is that of joining a conversation. When we had small children and sat down together to eat, the joy lay in the conversation. One child (I won't say which) would usually have a lot to say, while the other quietly got on with the serious business of eating. Prayer is a bit like those conversations. We're joining in a conversation around God's table. Sometimes we say too much, without listening; sometimes we're a bit tongue-tied, unsure what to say. The goal is to participate naturally, both speaking and listening, feeling at home in the company of God who loves us with a passion that's both fierce and tender, and who enjoys nothing more than spending time with us. Prayer is joining in the eternal conversation of the Trinity.

Perhaps our prayer needs to be less noisy and more about availability. There's a great thirst among Christians of all traditions today for more reflective forms of prayer, a desire to *encounter* God and not just *say things to* God. Ancient traditions are appearing in new clothes. I described some of these earlier: taking time with nature; *lectio divina*, which allows us to feed on Scripture rather than devour it; Ignatian meditation, which takes us right into the Gospels and to the feet of Jesus; the Examen, which gives us time to recognize where God has been and what God has been saying through the last 24 hours; centring prayer, which strips away the obstacles and lets God be God. These are the more contemplative ways in which Christians are finding reality and spiritual juice in their prayers, rather than formulas and duty.

And sometimes – not often but just occasionally – we can find ourselves so full of the Spirit that it's hard to know where the Spirit ends and we begin. Someone I know came out of work one day and was standing at the bus stop. She noticed the wind blowing listlessly through the trees as she waited, alone. An ordinary day. Soon, however, she became aware of an overwhelming sense of the divine presence in everything. The normal boundaries melted away; she was in everything and everything was in her. Every particle of creation appeared in 3D and HD, the wet ground glistening with light, everything more real than reality, more present than life itself. It was a disclosure of bliss that was to change her life fundamentally. Never again has she doubted the reality of God.

These mystical experiences are actually more common than our neatly packaged minds imagine. Paul, the rational theologian of the earliest churches, admitted to his own overwhelming moment of revelation in 2 Corinthians where he says of himself:

> I know a person in Christ who fourteen years ago was caught up to the third heaven – whether in the body or out of the body I do not know; God knows . . . And I know that such a person was caught up into Paradise and heard things that are not to be told . . . (2 Corinthians 12.2–4)

This was Paul the mystic, and he's not at all alone. We must be careful not to tread on people's dreams.

Prayer is therefore one way we encounter the Spirit who pervades all of life. Most of the time, however, we get on with the ordinary shopping list of life, where the Spirit is no less present. And here we hopefully encounter one of the loveliest outcomes of living in the flow of God's life: the fruit of the Spirit. The fruit of the Spirit, says Paul, is 'love, joy, peace, patience, kindness, generosity, faithfulness, gentleness, and self-control' (Galatians 5.22). It's a beautiful basket of fruit, one we can aspire to even if our current basket seems to be a bit hard and not quite ripe. I've lost count of the number of people I've met who've said faith started for them when someone in their life changed and became that kind of gracious person, displaying quite different qualities from the ones they were used to. This fruitfulness is deeply attractive.

The bad news is that fruit can't be tied on to our trees; it has to grow from the sap within, the sap of the Holy Spirit. Those who display these fruits make life taste good, in contrast to the rock-hard hedonism of those who make you want to stay under the duvet. The graciousness of a Spirit-led life is deeply refreshing to encounter and makes us want to grow more into the beauty of our own lives. It's all about having a living connection with Christ that produces fruit naturally. 'I am the vine, you are the branches. Those who abide in me and I in them bear much fruit, because apart from me you can do nothing' (John 15.5).

Let's be clear, the work of the Spirit is normal. It's not a freak occurrence. Certainly there can be experiences of the Spirit that take our breath away (and may indeed lead some people to speak in other tongues, like the disciples that first Day of Pentecost), but most of the work of the Spirit is beautifully mundane, lighting up our day with a touch of grace, enabling someone to cope with illness, nudging a friend who's looking for guidance, holding someone through a time of difficulty.

And let's not be possessive either. If God is at loose in the world and the Spirit really does fill up every space that comes available on the shoreline, then we can't keep the work of the Spirit only for believers. I don't know if she was a Christian or not, but after the tragic shooting of so many people at a concert in Las Vegas in 2017, a woman called Kimberly King said some interesting things when she was being interviewed. Her husband also survived, even though a bullet passed through his chest without hitting a main organ or artery, and she said this:

> There were 58 people who died, and I lived and my husband lived. If I don't do good in life from now on, and I don't live as if it was the last day, then it would be disrespectful to those people. All I want to do right now is help and be a greater person.

I would say that was evidence of the work of the Spirit of God, the Spirit, who permeates the life of the world. As they sing at Taizé: '*Ubi caritas et amor, deus ibi est*' – wherever there is charity and love, there God is present.

## The Spirit gives us resilience whatever life puts in our path

No lives are lived without crises. The smoothest lives are smooth only on the surface; underneath there usually is, or will have been, turbulence. I've always made it a rule to assume that everyone I meet is carrying a burden of some sort, I just don't know what it is. So I must tread gently. Of course, we long to spend our time on the sunlit mountain, just peace and silence and the wind in our hair, but life isn't like that. It's sharp rocks and icy winds and demented thunder, as well as love, friendship, and beauty beyond belief. So what's the role of the Spirit then, when the lights have gone out?

In an earlier chapter I quoted Julian of Norwich, the fourteenth-century mystic who had a series of 'showings' when she was ill and near to death. Reflecting on them later, she wrote the famous *Revelations of Divine Love*. Her words bear repetition in this context too. She clearly knew what it was like to share a bed with tragedy and she wasn't going to minimize the experience or pretend that there was some divine magic that would sort it out: 'God did not say, "You shall not be tempest-tossed, you shall not be work-weary, you shall not be discomforted." But he did say, "You shall not be overcome."'[3] That's a wonderful promise. The Spirit's gift is faithful resilience.

Desmond Tutu was once standing with a family as their home of many years was being bulldozed during the time of apartheid. The house contained all their precious family possessions. As the house was being crushed Desmond Tutu suggested they pray together, but then found he couldn't think of anything to say. There was silence, and then the man who owned the house prayed simply, 'We thank you, O God, that you love us.' That man was not overcome.

God isn't averse to miracles in hard situations. We see amazing things happen when we align ourselves with the flow of God's life. Synchronicities and coincidences start to happen that are nothing to do with being good or religious but rather to do with the flow of God's life being released within us. But there's no knowing how, where, when or why these new events become possible. In the meantime, however, we have an absolute guarantee about our safety in God. The promise of the Spirit is always, 'You shall not be overcome.'

Of course, it's possible that we are the cause of our own trauma and our conscience is just a small voice that makes minority reports that we routinely ignore. The job of the Spirit then might be to shout somewhat louder than usual. The singer Gloria Gaynor had a big hit with the song 'I Will Survive', which she recorded wearing a medical brace after emergency surgery following a bad fall. But as she became famous she also became careless of her health and well-being. She began partying hard and losing herself in drink and drugs. She says:

> One day, about 15 of us were having a party in our hotel suite and we were lying on the carpet. We were doing drugs and drinking when all of a sudden I felt someone grab me by the collar and pull me up, saying: 'That's enough.' I looked around and there was no one there. I was so shaken, I locked myself in the bathroom, saying, 'Oh my God,' over and over, until I realised that's who it was – God. I didn't party like that again.[4]

God the Spirit isn't always able to rescue us from our own folly in such fashion. However, we can be sure of God's never-leaving presence. And in that presence lies resilience, and in that resilience lies hope.

## The Spirit coaches us in Christlikeness

I have to admit to a strange addiction to the television programme *Strictly Come Dancing*. This is surprising, given that I'm the least likely Cha-Cha Champion or Samba Supremo you could imagine. What I find so compelling is how the professionals coach their unskilled celebrity partners into being accomplished dancers who achieve incredible proficiency. (There are exceptions to this, and the audience love them too.) The professional dancers take whoever they are given – making sure they look pleased – and then start working with the amateurs, encouraging, supporting, teaching, picking them up, stretching them further, never giving up. The celebrities become far better dancers than they ever believed possible. For me, it's a picture of the work of the Spirit in our lives.

The Spirit is a superb trainer. The goal we have before us is to follow Christ so closely that we become like him, and for that we need help. There's no silver bullet for becoming Christlike. The Spirit takes us just as we are, unskilled in the ways of holiness, and with infinite patience coaches us into being far more than we ever thought we could be. The Spirit encourages, supports, teaches, picks us up, stretches us further, never gives up. It's the task of a lifetime, and even then we've only just begun, but the joy of being increasingly conformed to the likeness of Christ is its own reward. With the Spirit as our partner, we learn the grace of the divine dance.

There's no escape on the dance floor; we are seen as we are, gliding or stumbling or somewhere in between. Similarly, there's no escape in the pursuit of Christlikeness. Greek temples were built for viewing from any of their four sides. Each side was equally beautiful and symmetrical. By contrast, Roman temples often only had one beautiful finished side, the front, while the other three were simply functional. Holiness involves four-sided integrity. There can be no masks that cover up darker truths.

Moreover, with the Holy Spirit working freely in the lives of Christians, hopefully there will be something that puzzles people and makes them wonder what makes these Christians tick. It might only be a fleeting encounter but they might recognize that here is someone who stands for a different set of values, a different world, and comes with deep reserves of love and grace that are strangely compelling. It's right that we should find this aspiration to be Christlike a huge challenge. But the Spirit is our 'professional coach' and has achieved remarkable transformations in countless lives, some of which we know.

The philosopher William James once wrote: 'In most of us, by the age of thirty, the character has set like plaster and will never soften again.' I know of only one answer to that dilemma, and that's the patient work of the Spirit within.

Let's return finally to the image I used earlier of the work of the Holy Spirit being like a symphony. This might be testing the metaphor to destruction, but the first work of the Spirit I mentioned was *the Spirit energizing God's people*, and this could be likened to the first movement of the symphony where the great theme is announced, full of energy and confidence. The second work of the Spirit was *the Spirit permeating all of life*, like the second movement with its serenity and peace. The third movement, the scherzo, is usually a lively, shorter piece, rather like *the Spirit giving us resilience whatever life puts in our path*. Last, the fourth movement draws everything together towards its final purpose and climax, just as *the Spirit patiently coaches us towards Christlikeness,* the goal of our lives as people of faith.

If that image stretches the reader's generosity too far, there's a précis in John 6.63 that will do very well indeed: 'It is the Spirit that gives life.'

# Tying it all together: how the five events made Christianity

On the last day of the pilgrimage we go to Abu Ghosh, one of the possible sites of Emmaus from Luke 24. The coach pulls up outside a high wall. We pile off. A cat wanders lazily away from this unwelcome commotion. We ring the bell and wait to be buzzed in. The gardens of this Benedictine community are beautifully green and peaceful and we wander contentedly through them, enjoying the shade, and then enter the basilica. Those Crusaders certainly knew how to build a church. The simple strength and serenity of the building is a gift to the soul. Its spare grandeur and perfect proportions make it the ideal place to bring the pilgrimage to a close.

It's also an excellent place to pull the threads of the experience together. Among the plethora of visits and experiences of the last ten days, five events have stood out like the massive columns of the Crusader church in which we're about to celebrate Communion – the birth in a Bethlehem cave, the death on a lonely hill, the resurrection in a quiet garden, the Ascension (somewhere), the coming of the Spirit in the upper city.

But what is the overall message of these events? How do they fit together around the enigmatic figure of Jesus, the prophet from Galilee? And how have these events made Christianity what it is today for over two billion people?

At its simplest, what we've been following is a love story with its origins in the nature of God who, we're told simply by John, is love (1 John 4.8). This love story can be told in two ways, one theological and the other personal. It's the biography of love and the biography of faith.

## The biography of love

The first chapter demonstrates that *love is creative by its very nature*. It always seeks ways to express itself, whether that be in the way a couple create a home together and perhaps nurture children within it, or in the way a writer's love of words leads to a first novel. A gardener's love of plants leads her to create a garden of delights, and a scientist's love of discovery leads her to create new answers to old problems. Love always creates in some form because the inner dynamic of love is centrifugal; it spins out into creativity.

God so loved the world he had made (and still makes) that an only Son was almost bound to emerge. It wasn't that God *had* to act in this way, more that God wanted to share what God is, wanted to share the life and joy. God's desire to communicate love and hope to humankind and to rescue us from ourselves led, therefore, to the incarnation, the 'enfleshment' of love in the person of Jesus. Nothing else could do it – no book, no theory, no declaration. It needed a person, and that person had to be so much on fire with the life of God that men and women would see God's ways in him, and hear God's words, and be released from their idols and addictions. This is the first chapter of the biography of love, the birth of Jesus.

The second chapter starts with *the extraordinary life of Jesus* around Galilee in which his teaching and preaching, his healings and his natural authority, had everyone sitting up, or racing to hear what he had to say. His message centred around the announcement of the kingdom of God, the reign of love, expressed in new ways that wove together love, justice and peace. This was dangerous and put the religious authorities on their guard. Such unlimited love was bound to be unsafe in a world like ours. The accuracy and power of this message about a new world order based on love became increasingly disturbing to both the religious and the secular leaders of the day and they eventually conspired to get rid of this dangerous Galilean. He was upsetting all the neatly constructed rules of behaviour that kept power in their hands. This man emitted too much light; it needed to be put out. In any case, people can't stand too much truth; it gets in the way of compromise and corruption. It has to be put in its place, with nails if necessary.

The third chapter in the biography of love starts *before dawn in a borrowed grave* outside the walls of Jerusalem. The dangerous Galilean was about to make a re-entry. It seems that a love like his is too full of life to stay dead. That kind of love is too powerful to kill off for good. Of course Jesus died, completely, but the kingdom of God that he demonstrated, the reign of love that he embodied, was raised by God to vindicate all that Jesus represented and all he had done. The resurrection was a huge surge of divine energy that threw the great engines of creation into reverse. Jesus lives, love has come again, and every negative and destructive force is put on notice.

The fourth chapter of the biography of love starts with *the puzzle of what you do with a love like this* that's exploded across creation. Almighty love had been let loose in the world and it had to be given its proper place. If the disciples were to do their work, they had to know where they were, and where Jesus was. Otherwise it was all confused. So the Ascension was the event that put everyone 'in their place' – Jesus at the right hand of the Father, and members of the new Jesus movement back in their own space, but as ambassadors of the sovereignty of Jesus. 'They . . . returned to Jerusalem with great joy; and they were continually in the temple blessing God' (Luke 24.52–53). Everything was all right, very much all right.

There was one thing missing, however. It was all very well going back to Jerusalem and blessing God in the Temple, but there was a bigger job to do now, getting out on the road with their new mandate, and the disciples didn't yet feel up to it. The fifth chapter therefore is about *God's answer to that problem* – simply to make the power of God's love available within the life of every believer. It was the coming of the Holy Spirit. And this transformational love of God isn't just for Christians and religious institutions, it's for a world deeply in need of change. The Spirit enables anyone to step into the immense flow of God's love and to cooperate with that divine energy in the renewing of the world – its people, its institutions, its inequalities, its suffering. This is a cause worth living and dying for.

Christians today are therefore either part of the fifth chapter, Pentecost, or they're writing the sixth, whichever way you want to look at it. It's the story of love – a love that is creative, redemptive and transformational. There's nothing sentimental about this love; it's tempered with steel. It's been through the fire of the cross and is offered to the world as its last, best and only hope. This is the biography of love and we retell it in whole or in part every Sunday as we gather as God's people in worship. In the Eucharist we recapitulate the story and reclaim its power in our lives. We're invited to let our story be absorbed into God's great story in such a way that God can continue to write his love into the world.

## The biography of faith

There's another way of telling the story of the five great events that made Christianity, and that's to see them as echoing the journey of faith that many people go on. This is not just the story of God's love in Jesus and what God was doing there; it's also in some ways the story of God's love in us, and what God is doing in us and in our love of God. What follows isn't meant to be in any way prescriptive. It simply describes the journey that many people of faith go on, if the experience of this pastor and spiritual accompanier is to be trusted. The journey goes like this.

The *birth of faith* happens in as many ways as there are believers. There are 'once-born' Christians who have always been aware of God's presence and love. Then there are 'twice-born' believers who have a special experience that brings them to faith and that probably remains an important touchstone and memory throughout their lives. There are also, I think, 'once-and-a-half-born' Christians who had a sort of faith but came to a fresh and much more meaningful knowledge of God later on. But whichever way it occurred, the baby lies in the manger; faith has been born.

We experience *a crisis of faith*. Hopefully this doesn't come for a while. Our faith needs time to grow beyond the manger, beyond even those Nazareth years. We need to grapple with the life and ministry of Jesus after he comes to Capernaum, and learn the ways of the kingdom so that we have some understanding of how to live faithfully in a complex world. But very often there comes a time when we have more questions than answers. We hit complexity. Objections to faith make some sense. Worship is dry. Prayer hits the ceiling. Conviction begins to drain away. Eventually this can become a full-scale crisis, and possibly no one knows what's going on because the mask has to be kept on at church. But the truth is that the life has gone out of our faith. This common experience corresponds in some ways to the Passion of Christ. Faith seems to be dying on the cross. For Jesus, after the comparative simplicity of Galilee where he could walk the sun-drenched paths, preach the kingdom, and see people healed and inspired, the darkness of Holy Week was a bitter experience. It can be like this for us too, as our previous gentle paddle down the river hits the rapids. Will our faith come through alive?

This leads to *new life in our faith*. The crisis is often a major breakpoint in the biography of faith. For some people it marks the point of departure from active Christian faith, or from any belief at all. There have been no answers, no light, no comfort, and we drift away from faith. For others this is the start of a refreshing new stage of faith, one that is more open, inclusive, generous and kind. An earlier stage of faith is often quite binary – right/wrong, yes/no, in/out. We may be suspicious of questions and doubt; we want certainty and clarity. And this may be an important stage of our faith journey, a necessary sorting out of what we believe when we live in a society so sceptical of faith. After the crisis, by contrast, our faith might seem to be less definite and clear-cut, but the truth is it's actually more deeply rooted. I often think I would go to the stake now for fewer things than I would have done at an earlier stage of life, but on the other hand what I take seriously now I take more seriously than ever. I'm less triumphalistic, and hopefully a better listener. I want to discuss rather than proclaim, engage rather than win. It's sometimes called a second naivety, a second simplicity that's gone through the fire and emerged with something even more important, more deeply etched into our very being. It's exciting to be set free in this way. It's a resurrection.

*Faith finds its true place in our lives.* The 'ascension' stage of our personal biography could be said to occur when we find that faith has settled into our lives in a way that both has clear priority and also feels natural. It's like a human relationship where the intense passion has quietened down and been replaced by a deep entwining of lives such that it's impossible to ever think of being apart. Faith isn't an add-on to an already well-structured life; it's the quiet central motor that constantly purrs away, supplying the energy, the values, the sense of meaning and purpose to our lives. This echoes the Ascension because it was when Jesus had departed from his 'now you see him, now you don't' post-resurrection life that the decks were cleared and the disciples knew where they were and what they had to do. Their calling was clear. Their faith was confident. So we too can come to that quiet assurance that God is God and has no hidden agenda, and that we can relax with this God in whom we trust and where we feel we belong. God is our home. Faith has found its true place in our lives.

*We are set free and empowered for action.* At an earlier stage of our faith journey we can easily become self-absorbed. We're trying to make sense of faith and how to be a Christian, how to pray and what we really believe, and it can all be pretty inward-looking. After going through a period of complexity or crisis (a 'cross-like' experience) and coming through to a stronger, deeper and less defensive faith (resurrection), and then discovering how central faith is to who we are and want to be (Ascension), we now, hopefully, come to see how the love that has overflowed into our lives in Jesus Christ must inevitably be passed on to others. It's our Pentecost. If we dam up the flow of love in ourselves, without letting it flow on to others, the result is that we get flooded and probably drown! The Spirit empowers the flow of love in, through and beyond us. We serve others with a grace that comes from the presence of the Spirit in us. We find that we are drawn into works of mercy and compassion, and to activities and organizations that in a huge number of different ways are building the foundations of the kingdom of God. This is our own Pentecost, a never-ending flow of the Spirit that empowers our love of God and our neighbour. It takes the rest of our lives.

The biography of faith I've outlined here is only indicative, in the sense that something like it happens to many people.

But there's no necessity to take these five 'chapters' in order or even to experience all of them. They may well repeat in some way, possibly in spiral form. It's important, however, that faith does make a journey and grows as it does so. If it gets stuck in its development it will inevitably diminish because the only sign of life is growth. Many people go through some period of complexity in their faith (not necessarily crisis) and without it they may not be motivated to go deeper. The danger is that we end up with a tight-knit set of beliefs and practices that look more like rules, regulations and rituals than relationship, more like law than grace.

The Holy Land, or more properly the Land of the Holy One, is a wonderful place to reflect on the five events that made Christianity, but we don't need to go there to do so. Serapion the Sindonite, a fourth-century monk, went on pilgrimage to Rome. There he was told of a famous recluse who never left her room. He was fascinated by this as he was a great traveller, so he called on her and asked her, 'Why do you just sit here all the time?' She replied, 'I'm not sitting. I'm on a journey.' The most significant journeys are those of the mind and spirit.

My hope is that perhaps we can now see a little more clearly how these five events all make sense, how they make one story in five chapters. The one story is called the Biography of Love. Being a Christian isn't about obeying the rules or saying the creed with your fingers crossed. It's about following the main character in the Biography of Love, and trusting the Author of the book.

And in that confidence we can get on with enjoying the sequel – the Biography of Faith – and being changed, infinitely slowly, so slowly we may not even notice, into the likeness of Christ.

# Questions for group discussion or personal reflection

The best questions will be your own, because you know your group and what works best for them. But here are some suggestions to get you started. The questions are grouped under the five events rather than under each chapter, and therefore envisage five sessions, but they could be split up by chapter if a longer course is intended.

You might want to choose a few of the questions rather than tackle them all. Or you might want to read through them and then reframe them more appropriately for your group. Or you might want to read through them and start again!

The 'starter question' is meant to be a more general way into the subject. The page numbers in brackets show what parts of the book the questions relate to.

## The birth

*Starter:* What were, or are, your favourite ways of celebrating the Christian heart of Christmas?

1 How important is it to you that Mary was a virgin or that Jesus was born in a stable?
2 Do you tend to think of the divinity of Jesus from the top down or the bottom up (p. 19)?
3 What do you make of the two descriptions of Jesus on pp. 20 and 21?
4 Are you happy with Jesus having those very human emotions described on p. 23?
5 As a group, list the number of ways in which local Christians are committed to helping make life better for individuals and groups within the community. And be surprised (p. 31)!

6 How easy is it to admit vulnerability in your family, with friends, at church (p. 34)?
7 When have you had that experience of 'not being overcome' (p. 36)?

## The killing

*Starter.* Does the idea of going to Jerusalem attract you? Why, or why not? See if anyone in the group has been to Jerusalem. If so, how did they cope with the mayhem of the city when they were trying to be on a thoughtful pilgrimage?

1 Love as substitute, as example, as victor, as participation in God's big story. Do these ideas help you to understand the cross (pp. 47–60)? (Each one of these could be taken separately.)
2 What would be your 30-second explanation of the cross to someone who had never encountered the story?
3 How can we 'make love a way of life' (p. 62)?
4 How, actually, does God's suffering help us with ours (p. 64)?
5 Have you known, or known of, people who have clearly been released from addictions and negative habits by coming to faith (p. 66)?
6 How 'successful' have you been at forgiveness and reconciliation (p. 68)?
7 Have you known people who have so handed over their lives that they have 'disappeared into Christ' (p. 71)? Who have been the saints of your life experience?

## The manhunt

*Starter.* Who do you identify with in the resurrection stories?

1 What excites you about the resurrection of Jesus?
2 Do you find the arguments for the empty tomb and the appearances of Jesus convincing (pp. 76–8)?
3 How would you say you 'experience' the risen Christ (p. 81)?
4 How do you react to the huge claim of Tom Wright that the resurrection brings in a new creation, or of Rowan Williams that the resurrection is like 'a second Big Bang' (pp. 88, 89)?

5 Where do you think the Church can take credit for advancing social change, and where is it lagging behind (pp. 97ff.)?
6 Do you approach death confidently (p. 99)?
7 How does your church show that it's motivated and inspired by the resurrection? Does it have the character of Christ (p. 101)?

## The leaver who remained

*Starter:* Do you usually go to an Ascension Day service? Why, or why not?

1 How do you see/imagine/understand the event we call the Ascension (pp. 104–6)?
2 What are the alternative 'lords' in contemporary culture (p. 109)? Is it possible to subvert them?
3 What does it mean to you to say that 'He's got the whole world in his hands' (p. 112)?
4 Is the idea of the ascended Christ too dazzling to be of much use (p. 116)?
5 'We have a clear job description' (p. 117). What do you think yours is?
6 Do you recognize the experience of being 'speechless before God' (p. 120)? Would (or do) any of the suggestions on pp. 121–3 help?

## The promise

*Starter:* Does your church have any special traditions for Pentecost or have you any memories of these from other times and places?

1 What does Pentecost mean to you? Try to get beyond conventional phrases and speak out of your personal experience (p. 128).
2 Ask the group to name the gifts they see in each other. Then ask each member to respond and also name the gifts they think they've been given (which may or may not be the same as those others have named).

3 Do we claim too much by saying that 'everything has changed', when the world remains in such a mess (p. 131)? How far would you go in agreeing?

4 How does the idea of God as Trinity help your thinking about God (p. 132)?

5 Are you content with the idea that the Spirit permeates all of life, not just the lives of believers? Why (p. 137)?

6 Do you like the image of prayer as joining a conversation (p. 138)? How would you develop that image further?

7 How do you measure Christlikeness (p. 142)? That is, if you were to think someone had grown in Christlikeness, how would you recognize that?

# *Notes*

## 1 A word at the beginning

1 Walter Brueggemann, *Finally Comes the Poet* (Minneapolis, MN: Fortress Press, 1990).
2 Justin Welby, interview at St Mellitus College, December 2013.
3 Paul Kalanithi, *When Breath Becomes Air* (London: Vintage, 2016), pp. 168–71.
4 *The Week*, 2 December 2016.

## 2 The birth: what happened?

1 Paula Gooder, *Journey to the Manger* (Norwich: Canterbury Press, 2015), p. 101.
2 Peter Walker, *In the Steps of Jesus* (Oxford: Lion Hudson, 2009), p. 22.

## 3 The birth: what does it mean?

1 Richard Rohr, *Daily Meditation*, 19 January 2018.
2 Bishop James Bell, sermon at the funeral of Bishop David Jenkins, Durham Cathedral, 28 September 2016.
3 Rowan Williams, *Tokens of Trust* (Norwich: Canterbury Press, 2007), p. 57.
4 Lord Hailsham, *The Door Wherein I Went* (London: Collins, 1975), pp. 54–5.
5 Sam Wells, *Incarnational Ministry* (Norwich: Canterbury Press, 2017).

## 4 The birth: what does it mean for us now?

1 Tina Beattie, *The New Atheists* (London: Darton, Longman and Todd, 2007), p. 169.
2 Julian of Norwich, *Revelations of Divine Love*, chapter 68.

## 6 The killing: what does it mean?

1 Rowan Williams, *God with Us* (London: SPCK, 2017), p. 4.
2 Quoted in Richard Rohr, *Things Hidden* (Cincinnati, OH: St Anthony Messenger Press, 2007), p. 186.
3 Helen Waddell, *Peter Abelard* (London: Constable, 1933), p. 270.
4 Shusaku Endo, *Silence* (London: Marylebone House, 2016), pp. 261–4.
5 Gustaf Aulén, *Christus Victor* (London: SPCK, 2010).
6 Ronald Rolheiser, *The Passion and the Cross* (London: Hodder and Stoughton, 2015), p. 69.
7 Sam Wells, *A Nazareth Manifesto* (Oxford: Wiley-Blackwell, 2015), p. 239.

## 7 The killing: what does it mean for us now?

1 Alan Hargrave, *One for Sorrow* (London: SPCK, 2017), p. 45.
2 Geoffrey Studdert Kennedy, *The Word and the Work* (London: Longmans, 1925), pp. 57–8.
3 Herbert McCabe, source untraced.
4 Mark Oakley, *The Splash of Words* (Norwich: Canterbury Press, 2016), p. 26.

## 8 The manhunt: what happened?

1 David Ford, *The Shape of Living* (Norwich: Canterbury Press, 2012), p. 160.
2 Albert Schweitzer, *The Quest of the Historical Jesus* (1910), conclusion.

## 9 The manhunt: what does it mean?

1 Malcolm Guite, *The Word in the Wilderness* (Norwich: Canterbury Press, 2014), p. 8.
2 C. S. Lewis, *Miracles* (first published 1947).
3 Bertrand Russell, *Autobiography* (London: Psychology Press), p. 393.
4 Tom Wright, sermon preached in Durham Cathedral, April 2007.
5 Rowan Williams, *Tokens of Trust* (Norwich: Canterbury Press, 2007), p. 95.

## 10 The manhunt: what does it mean for us now?

1 Gerard Manley Hopkins, 'The Wreck of the Deutschland'.

2 J. R. R. Tolkien, *The Lord of the Rings* (London: George Allen and Unwin, 1954).

3 J. R. R. Tolkien, 'On Fairy Stories', essay (1939).

4 John V. Taylor, *A Matter of Life and Death* (London: SCM Press, 1986), p. 18.

5 Ronald Rolheiser, *The Passion and the Cross* (London: Hodder and Stoughton, 2015), p.124.

6 John Shea, quoted in Rolheiser, *The Passion and the Cross*, p. 131.

## 11 The leaver who remained: what happened?

1 Michael Lloyd, *Café Theology* (London: St Paul's Theological Centre, 2012), p. 235.

2 C. S. Lewis, *Miracles* (first published 1947).

## 12 The leaver who remained: what does it mean?

1 Martin Laird, *Into the Silent Land* (London: Darton, Longman and Todd, 2005), p. 11.

2 Bill Bryson, *The Road to Little Dribbling* (London: Transworld, 2015), p. 357.

3 Julian of Norwich, *Revelations of Divine Love*, chapter 86.

4 For a full discussion of this see John V. Taylor, *The Christlike God* (London: SCM Press, 1992), chapters 7 and 8.

## 13 The leaver who remained: what does it mean for us now?

1 Geoffrey Howard, *Dare to Break Bread* (Manchester: Pendlebury Press, 2017), p. 66.

## 14 The promise: what happened?

1 Mark Oakley, *A Good Year* (London: SPCK, 2017), p. xxiii.

## 15 The promise: what does it mean?

1 Rupert Shortt, *God Is No Thing* (London: Hurst and Co., 2016), p. 67.

2 John V. Taylor, *The Go-Between God* (London: SCM Press, 1972).

## 16 The promise: what does it mean for us now?

1 Michael Lloyd, *Café Theology* (London: St Paul's Theological Centre, 2012), p. 252.

2 John V. Taylor, *The Go-Between God* (London: SCM Press, 1972), p. 17.

3 Julian of Norwich, *Revelations of Divine Love*, chapter 68.

4 *The Week*, 20 May 2017.